John Watts De Peyster

A Vindication of James Hepburn

Fourth earl of Bothwell, third husband of Mary, Queen of Scots

John Watts De Peyster

A Vindication of James Hepburn
Fourth earl of Bothwell, third husband of Mary, Queen of Scots

ISBN/EAN: 9783337322939

Printed in Europe, USA, Canada, Australia, Japan

Cover: Foto ©ninafisch / pixelio.de

More available books at **www.hansebooks.com**

VINDICATION

OF

JAMES HEPBURN,

FOURTH EARL OF BOTHWELL,

THIRD HUSBAND

OF

MARY, QUEEN OF SCOTS.

"KIEP TREST" (*Be Faithful*).—BOTHWELL'S MOTTO.

"ARE THESE THINGS SO?"—*The Acts*, vii. 1.

"*Neither can they prove the things whereof they now accuse me.*"—THE ACTS, xxiv. 13.

"With him his Fortune played as with a ball,
She first has tossed him up, and now she lets him fall."
Verses on Medallion of COUNT GRIFFENFELD, Royal Library, Copenhagen.

BY

J. WATTS DE PEYSTER,

"ANCHOR."

PHILADELPHIA, PA.:
L. R. HAMERSLY & CO.,
1510 CHESTNUT STREET.
1882.

JAMES HEPBURN, EARL OF BOTHWELL,[1]

THIRD HUSBAND OF MARY, QUEEN OF SCOTS.

———————

> " But who that Chief?—His name on every shore
> Is famed and fear'd—they ask, and know no more.
> With these he mingles not but to command ;
> Few are his words, but keen his eye and hand.
> Ne'er seasons he with mirth their jovial mess,
> But they forgive his silence for success.
>   *   *   *   *   *   *
> ' Steer to that shore !'—they sail. ' Do this !'—'tis done.
> ' Now form and follow me !'—the spoil is won.
> Thus prompt his accents and his actions still,
> And all obey, and few inquire his will.
>   *   *   *   *   *   *
> Yet they repine not, so that Conrad [2] guides ;
> And who dare question aught that he decides ?
>   *   *   *   *   *   *
> Still sways their souls with that commanding art
> That dazzles, leads, yet chills the vulgar heart.
> What is that spell that thus his lawless train
> Confess and envy, yet oppose in vain?
> What should it be that thus their faith can bind ?
> *The power of Thought,—the magic of the Mind !*
> Linked with success, assumed and kept with skill,
> That moulds another's weakness to its will ;
> Wields with their hands, but, still to these unknown,
> Makes even their mightiest deeds appear his own.
> Such hath it been, shall be, beneath the sun,—
> The many still must labor for the one !
> 'Tis Nature's doom ; but let the wretch who toils
> Accuse not, hate not him who wears the spoils.
> Oh ! if he knew the weight of splendid chains,
> How light the balance of his humbler pains !"
> Byron's " Corsair," ¶¶ ii., viii.

[1] Curious to say, this name or title of Bothwell was spelled in documents of the time in twenty-four different ways.

[2] Alphonse de Lamartine, in his " Marie Stuart," or " Regina," says that Byron predicated his poem, " The Corsair," on the maritime career of Bothwell, Lord High Admiral of Scotland, with whose wife, Lady Jane Gordon (divorced to enable the Earl to marry Mary Stuart), the poet was indirectly connected through his mother's ancestry. See letters of Sir Gilbert Elliot (first Earl of Minto, 1, 2, note and 24, note), said to be kin, by some line of descent, with John Elliot, of the

There are few facts in history which are so startling as the general ignorance of the reading classes as to the real portraiture of some of the most remarkable characters who in so many cases have influenced nations, and in a few instances the world. These few resemble mountains like Ararat, which until within a few years have scarcely been explored at all, and have only been ascended by a small group of daring men. There are others, again, like Mount St. Elias, that loom up through centuries as that volcano is visible for an immense distance, yet has neither been climbed nor examined. In many respects the greatest man in history, with the exception of St. Paul, was Hannibal, and yet how very, very little is known of him except through his enemies, whose instincts and interests compelled a misrepresentation of him. It is true that in his case his own language, not only as a living and a dead one,—*i.e.*, in speech and writing,—and every exemplar of the Punic records, has perished from the face of the earth. He wrote his name, however, in blood and desolation so indelibly that his victories and his stratagems are "Household Words." The proverb "*Hannibal ad portas*" still signifies the presence of a terror imminent and dreadful. His wisdom, his virtues, how few are aware of them! And yet in both he was as pre-eminent as in valor and victory. He was a victim of the "Irony of Fate" and of the vices and virulence of political faction. He was greatest when no longer victorious, and the expression "Hannibal's Ring" signifies at once the refuge of despair and the ever-ready resource by which escape is only possible from the meanness and malice of triumphant enmity. Like the greatest Carthaginian, the greatest German, Frederick the Nonpareil, carried ever with him poison in a ring, determined not to survive the last humiliation. Hannibal was compelled to use it, Frederick was not. God *willed it to be so.* That is the only possible explanation.

Another of the same unhappy class is Richard III. of England. His character is the synonym for all that is bad except cowardice. Is this the true verdict?

> "No! by St. Bride of Bothwell! No!"

The exact reverse is most probably the fact. Whence, then, is the popular and erroneous opinion derived? From Shakspeare's tragedy.

Park, the celebrated Borderer or Outlaw, who claimed to be, if not the head of his name, at least the chief of a powerful branch of the Elliots, and by hereditary right Captain of Hermitage Castle, and who was killed in a personal encounter with Bothwell near Hermitage Castle, in Liddelsdale.

This way of judging Bothwell from the nineteenth century standpoint of morality is ridiculous. He must be judged or gauged by his times. Some of the worthies of England were pirates, as he is falsely charged to have been, or, worse, abettors of piracy, sharing proceeds but not dangers. Hawkins, a great English admiral, was a kidnapper of negroes and father of the English-African slave-trade.

Was Shakspeare honest in his convictions? There are many reasons to believe he was not. He was a courtier. His success depended on the favor of a circle of influential men, who themselves were neither more nor less than sycophants of a Queen whose favorite food was fulsome flattery. No extreme of that cloying sweetness was unpalatable. Richard III. was the head of the House of York, Elizabeth's grandfather of the House of Lancaster. Richard had been one of the most potent factors in the Wars of the Roses, which for twenty-four years drove forth the Lancasterian Line and occupied their throne. If Richard was the rightful monarch, Henry VII. was a rebel and a usurper, and Elizabeth, branded with bastardy by a party at home and a creed everywhere, was likewise not the legitimate tenant of her royal seat. Shakspeare did not dare to do Richard justice, and his genius, perverted in this instance to a cruel crime, painted his historical picture to please the woman who wielded the sceptre with more than ordinary masculine force. The great Marlborough stated that all that he knew of English history was derived from Shakspeare's plays. How many who would not admit this truth are nevertheless under the same mesmeric influence? Physically Richard was not the deformity of popular conception. In many respects he was handsome. His mental gifts have never been denied. His intelligence was very extraordinary. In every kind of courage he was a hero. What remains to be examined? His morals. By what rule are they to be judged? His own dark era, or by the present of electric lights? The writer has examined several works which completely clear Richard from the crimes imputed to him. As was said of Louis Philippe, years after he was driven forth, "France will yet inscribe him among her good kings." Had Richard conquered at Bosworth Field, there is little question but that instead of being condemned he would have been "crowned"—to use the word in the French sense in regard to a successful competitor in art, science, or general literature—by posterity. These preliminary remarks must serve as a preface to the subject of this article, James Hepburn, Earl of Bothwell. The intention has been to lead up, step by step, the reader's attention to the consideration that follows. The Battle of Bosworth was fought 22d August, 1485. Just eighty-two years afterwards an engagement occurred in Scotland, at Carberry Hill, 15th June, 1567, which was equally decisive of the ascendency of two men, James Hepburn, Earl of Bothwell, and James Stuart, Earl of Murray. The former, the most manly, like Richard III., lost his cause, and, like the Yorkist scion also, has been handed down to posterity blackened and blasted by a fury of obloquy as entirely false as utterly undeserved in many respects. The latter, like Henry VII., was as cunning as a fox, ever "looking through his fingers" at evil deeds by which he expected to profit without exposing his fingers to the heat by which the chestnuts for his eating were being roasted. It was not until over three centuries had elapsed that Bothwell found a defender, one Dr. Petrick, who published in German (imprint, Berlin and St. Petersburg, 1874) a complete vindication of Bothwell, which, strange to say, agrees not only in idea and expression, but often in the very words with the views taken by the writer, as set forth in "A Study : Mary, Queen of Scots," published at New York in February, 1882. With the indefatigable research of a German critic,—in this respect unexceeded and seldom equaled by historical investigators in other countries,—with an analysis of animus, argument, anecdote, allusion, and authorities worthy a chemist in search of arsenic in a corpse, and with the logic of an experienced lawyer, Dr. Petrick demolishes the corrupt testimony on which Bothwell has been condemned, and accumulates rebutting evidence on which he must be acquitted. If ever there was an ambitious, hypocritical, astute, and bold competitor for sovereign power, from which he was debarred by illegitimate birth, it was this Earl of Murray. Subservient to the clergy through policy, he found it the best investment of his life, and it served him not only while he lived, but has been equally precious to his memory. With their long black cloaks Knox and the preachers covered him, stained with political crimes, from the stigma of individual fraud, and calculated personal ingratitude to his forgiving sister, Queen Mary, and veiled the truth from the eyes of the people, and then threw their sanctimonious robes over his corpse, as a similar protection to his reputation, after he had been shot by Bothwellhaugh.

Murray was the favorite of the clergy, who are evil cattle to provoke, and invaluable friends if cunningly cultivated. Charles Martel preserved France from Mahometanism, but taxed the priesthood for the benefit of the troops which enabled him to triumph, and the priests consigned the savior of Western Christendom to eternal fire, obloquy, and misrepresentation. The Puritans and their descendants wrote the history of the United States, and they arrogate to New England the origin of a greatness due far more to New York and Hollandish-Huguenot influence. Even so it was with Bothwell. The parties he opposed in policy and in arms have furnished the particulars of his story.

One of the recent German biographers of Mary remarks that the blacker Mary's champions succeed in painting Bothwell the whiter they hope thereby to make Mary appear; but here is a fit application of the motto selected by the Marquis de Nadaillac for his great work, "Les Premiers Hommes et les Temps préhistoriques," "Facta non Verba," adding (ii. 463, (1)), "Abuse is never argument, and it has always seemed to me that those who resort to abuse as a weapon do so because they have nothing more available."

And here let it be remarked, although in a measure out of place, but for emphasis, scarcely one who united in betraying Mary and

Bothwell but expiated their sins by the assassin's bullet, in brawl or battle, on the scaffold by the cord or axe, in the gloom of a cell or a dungeon, or some other unnatural end.

Every human being is a product! Mary was the natural result of ancestry, education, elevation, time, place, and circumstance. The same remarks apply to Bothwell. Mary was not a worse woman than her grandmother, her mother-in-law, her sister-in-law, nor the majority of the ladies by position in France and in Scotland. To judge her by public opinion to-day would be just as reasonable as to subject the Bishops in Scotland just prior to her accession to the same touchstone that would be applied to the private and public life of a prominent clergyman in the Middle States at present. Burton is almost stunning in his revelations of the morals of the spiritual as well as temporal aristocracy of Scotland at that time. He tells us (iii. 186) during the reign of James V., father of Mary, "A great tide of profligacy had then set in upon Scotland, and the clergy were the leaders in it." "Priests," said Garibaldi, "are [and have been, in many instances] the greatest scourges of mankind." True! Aye!

"Some families (he adds, iii. 308-9) of the poorer landed gentry held in relation to churchmen a position that could not but subject them to humiliation. Their sisters or daughters were the known concubines of rich ecclesiastics, and held rank accordingly. For many of the clergy who lived in concubinage, according to the letter of the law, there was doubtless the plea that morally they led a life of married domesticity. . . . Every man who practiced it was a law unto himself. There was no distinct sanction drawing, as the law of marriage draws, an obvious, unmistakable line between domesticity and profligacy."

"And of many of the great, rich churchmen, such as Cardinal Beaton and his successor, it was known that they did not profess these humble domestic views, or place themselves in the position of dissenters from the Church, by affecting the life of married persons. They flared their amours in the face of the world, as if proud of the excellence of their taste for beauty and the rank and birth that had become prostrate to their solicitations. It seemed as if their very greatness as temporal grandees enabled them to defy the ordinary laws of decorum, while their spiritual rank secured to them immunity from that clerical punishment which it was their duty to pronounce against less gifted sinners."

If professed moralists were to undertake to apply the elastic laws of Moses and the real interpretation of the Seventh Commandment to the lives of Scottish magnates, and contrast Bothwell with those who ought to have set an example, they would have to pronounce a merciful judgment on him.

Mary Stuart—to whom might be applied with more real justice than to the lady for whom they were originally intended the lines of Alfieri, addressed to his beloved Louisa, Countess of Albany:

" Bright are the dark locks of her braided hair,
　　Grecian her brow, its silken eyebrows brown ;
　　Her eyes—oh, lover, to describe forbear—
　　Life can their glance impart, and death their frown !
　　Her mouth no rosebud, and no rose her cheek
　　May emulate in freshness, fragrance, hue ;
　　A voice so soft and sweet to hear her speak
　　Inspires delight and pleasures ever new ;
　　A smile to soothe all passions save despair ;
　　A slight and graceful form ; a neck of snow ;
　　A soft white hand, and polished arm as fair ;
　　A foot whose traces Love delights to show ;
　　And with these outward charms, which all adore,
　　A mind and heart more pure and perfect given ;
　　For thee thy lover can desire no more,
　　Adorned by every grace and gift of Heaven."

—Mary Stuart, the Fate of Bothwell, was a conscienceless flirt, but
not altogether the bad woman that all but her devoted champions conclude. She was a good wife to her first husband, Francis II. The
very ardor of her love killed him. After his death she had fancies,
guilty in some senses, but not criminal. It is very likely that in the
early time of her widowhood she had a sneaking kindness for Bothwell.
The French proverb, " To agree too well is sometimes dangerous," applied to their case. Darnley, who made a trip to France in the wild
hope of winning her, soon after Francis died, she would not look at. She
preferred D'Amville, one of the noblest Frenchmen of the day, who was
in love with her. He was married. It is insinuated that a suggestion
was made to him that the obstacle of a wife might be easily removed.
In spite of his passion he was a gallant gentleman, and tore himself
away from the temptation. Chastelar and Gordon were fancies. Mary
did not hesitate, as do most women of her kind, to sacrifice both to expediency, the first as a sop to public opinion, suspicions in regard to
herself, and the second to the momentary pressure of politics. " What
a pity," cried Knox, " the de'il should ha'e his abode in sic' a piece of
bonnie painted clay !"　" Mary," quoth Laurie Todd, " was a deep, dis-
sembling, polite woman."

" Bathsheba's [Mary's] was an impulsive nature under a deliberative
aspect. An Elizabeth in brain and a Mary Stuart in spirit, she often
performed actions of the greatest temerity with a manner of extreme
discretion. Many of her thoughts were perfect syllogisms ; unluckily
they always remained thoughts. Only a few were irrational assump-
tions, but, unfortunately, they were the ones which most frequently
grew into deeds." The Duke d'Aumale, in his " History of the
Condés," styles her justly the " MEDUSA OF BEAUTIES,"—admirable,
perfect comparison ; excellent. " Ada [Mary] is the magnetic mountain
of the Fairy Tale : she attracts every one ; every one is wrecked, burned.
She has nerves of steel and a heart of granite."

" How many of our special views and consequent acts, for instance, arose from the accident of birth, the opinions of those among whom we are educated, and so on." " Man's interference with nature" is never successful. " As is well known, Nature never corrects herself." " What a confused mixture of malice and feminine weakness" was Mary. "Let a woman's heart seem ever so cold, glacier flowers will ever be found on it." " In love great pleasures jostle great sorrows." " No man's soul is alone,—Laocoon or Tobit,—the serpent has it by the heart or the angel by the hand." " All the joints of his [Bothwell's or Mary's] life were torn, dislocated by these strong horses of Fate tied to his vitals and pulling in different ways." Darnley captured her in a moment of weakness, and her desire for him flashed up into flame as soon as she was caught, through the eye, by his physical graces and training. He was handfasted to her early in April, 1566, but not actually married until 29th of July following. Meanwhile they lived on the most intimate terms. After marriage her love was extinguished almost as suddenly as it had been enkindled, by his weakness and vileness. All this time there is a strange, sometimes strikingly evident, and at others almost imperceptible, thread, fine as silk, but strong as Fate, connecting her with Bothwell. When at length her passion for this " REAL MAN" took possession of her, the long pent-up flood burst every barrier, and bore her away with it as helpless as an ice dam, which, between heat and freshet, is first crushed or broken down, then torn away, and finally borne off shattered and shattering by the raging stream. *Every human being is a product!* Not to trace cause and effect beyond her grandparents, what was her grandfather, James IV.? (Burton, iii. 80–81.) " He was one who pleased the world and bought golden opinions from it, diverting censure from his failings, which were many and flagrant. He was a libertine, and that in a form which was likely to set the fashion in that direction, one of the direst mischiefs which a king can do to a people; for, however self-willed they may be and disinclined to submission, a sovereign can always make himself the absolute lord of fashion. The same failings in his father were dealt with severely and scornfully, and a favorite mistress was bandied among the people by the contemptuous name of the ' Daisy.' This was the result of the sordid and unroyal ways of that king. The son's mistresses are seen in succession passing in splendor before an admiring people. At the beginning of his reign, while he is yet but a boy, his mistress, Lady Margaret Drummond, comes on the stage conspicuous in her grandeur, to become still more conspicuous in her fate; for she and her sister died together at Drummond Castle, so suddenly and in such a manner as to convince all that poison had been at work."

What was her grandmother, Margaret of Lancaster, worthy sister of Henry VIII. of England? The marriage tie sat very lightly upon her. The story of her marriages and divorces, repeated and

glaring, have been too often related to need repetition here. One of
her fancies, however, is seldom alluded to, and yet it must have been
patent, because it is the subject of a picture reproduced in Pinkerton's
"Scottish Gallery." It represents Margaret and the Duke of Albany,
Regent of Scotland, together, and is supposed to have been painted in
1522, when the connection became notorious, and her brother, Henry
VIII., and Cardinal Wolsey loudly accused her of adultery. Between
the faces a butterfly is painted, the indication of "*an amour voltige,*"
to which a guard or attendant behind the queen is pointing with his
finger. This fine picture, probably painted in the north of England,
is half satiric and political. Margaret's husband, Angus, was in the
English interest; Albany, her temporary lover, always in the French;
and thus it was some English artist gave vent to his feelings against
the determined opponent of his country. James V. was certainly as
loose in his morals as his father and his mother. Burton says "He
would, according to modern notions, be called a profligate." He left
behind him six illegitimate children, amply endowed and highly placed,
besides a number not acknowledged. The best known of those six was
James Stuart, at first Prior of St. Andrew's, then Earl of Murray, and
finally Regent of Scotland. Very extensive reading discovers no direct
charge against Mary of Guise, Mary's mother, but she was of the
house of Lorraine, in whose veins, prince or prelate, the blood flowed
fiercely and furiously. Somewhere it is hinted that she stood in a peculiar relation to the magnificent Cardinal Beaton, and undoubtedly she
did considerable flirting with Bothwell's father, if not more. These
were the times and manners that justified such verses as Scott's, in his
"Bridals of Triermain," Canto II., ¶ XVIII,—

> "And still these lovers' fame survives,
>   For faith so constant shown:
> There were two who loved their neighbors' wives,
>   And one who loved his own."

To this the author adds as a note an extract from Ascham's "School-
master," written about the time of Mary's birth: "In our forefathers'
tyme, when Papistrie, as a standyng poole, covered and overflowed all
England, fewe books were read in our tongue, savying certaine bookes
of chevalrie, as they said, for pastime and pleasure; which, as some
say, were made in the monasteries by idle monks or wanton chanons.
As one, for example, 'La Morte d'Arthure;' the whole pleasure of
which book standeth in two speciale poynts—in open manslaughter and
bold bawdrye; in which booke they be counted the noblest knightes
that do kill most men without any quarrell, and commit fowlest adoul-
teries by sutlest shiftes; as Sir Launcelot, with the wife of King
Arthur, his master; Sir Triestram with the wife of King Marke, his
uncle; Sir Lameracke, with the wife of King Lote; that was his own

aunt. This is good stuffe for wise men to laugh at, or honest men to take pleasure at, yet I know when God's Bible was banished the court, and La Morte d'Arthure received into the prince's chamber."

Murray[3] was not a profligate like his father and mother. He was too cold and calculating a mortal to risk the moral support of the reformers and staid middle classes by open indulgence in illicit pleasures. Can his greatest admirers deny, however, that he was blind to every kind of profligacy in those whose support he sought or continued to be necessary to him after it was acquired? He was too astute to commit crimes. He winked at them, and his winks were often equivalent to State warrants; sometimes to kill reputations, at others to hale into prison or drive forth into exile, or even to lead to execution. " He looked through his fingers" at the murder of Rizzio, at the assassination of Darnley; at the incarceration of his sister Mary. He always slunk away when a bad deed was doing and done; he always turned up most opportunely when the benefits of it were to be secured. He always turned at a crisis

> " To Morton, steeped in lust and guilt,
> My old accomplice he."

Morton, his particular associate, in some respects his *alter ego*, was a cold-blooded profligate. Rich or poor, gentle or plebeian, if he saw a woman that pleased him, he rarely failed to possess himself of her. Among a nobility whose almost only redeeming quality was personal bravery, to whom oaths were trifles as light as air, associations, "bonds," or "bands" blanks after signature or the subscribers' purposes were attained, honor a by-word, truth a jest, conscience an unknown quantity, Bothwell, if he was comparatively pure and honest, as he is known to have been, among such creatures, black as sin could make them, he must have appeared like a white crow. That he was "a REAL

---

[3] " At the head [of the Lords of the Congregation, Protestant nobility] was Lord James Stuart, Prior of St. Andrew's, better known as the Earl of Murray, a bastard brother of the queen, formidable alike from his ability and his ambition. He was the natural son of James V. by Margaret, daughter of Lord Erskine, and is believed, from an early period of his life, to have entertained the hope of obtaining a reversal of his illegitimacy, in which case he might, in the event of Mary dying without issue, have advanced a claim to the crown of Scotland. Nor was this a scheme so wild as to appear beyond the pale of probability. The claims of Henry VII. to the throne of England had been rested upon no better foundation, and Elizabeth's right . . . was worse than doubtful Murray was just the kind of man likely to succeed in such a design. He was cool, cautious, long-sighted, and unscrupulous; and by taking the popular side in the then all-absorbing religious controversy he greatly increased his reputation and his power. He also entered into deep and intricate relations with the Court of England.

" Murray has by more than one writer been represented as a high-minded and patriotic man. Before Elizabeth he was no better than a spaniel, cowering under the degradation of the lash, which was often unsparingly applied."—*Aytoun's " Bothwell,"* 197, 202-3.

MAN" ("*wahre Mann*") as Petrick styles him, loyal, patriotic, able, faithful to his trusts, brave as his sword, in such an evil time and generation, is sufficient to excuse a love of wassail which he never allowed to overcome his senses, of women whom he never permitted to interfere with duty, or a wrath which in most instances was not only just in its object but justified in its means.   Hosack, who championed Mary with the zeal of a knight and the professional ardor and ability of a practiced lawyer, who is no friend to Bothwell, is nevertheless compelled to concede to him characteristics which make him loom up like a "real man" and a true Scotchman, even as Pompey's Pillar towers above the Arab huts and the ruins and desolation that surround it.

Mary wrote, after her marriage, to the French court that "among her Scotch nobility she had not found one who could enter into a comparison with the Earl of Bothwell, either in the elevation (*reputation*) of his house or lineage, his own personal merits, his wisdom, his valor, and that she had yielded with the utmost willingness to the desire of the 'Three Estates' in espousing him." This is as grand and sufficient as a more recent letter of a noble lady to her knight under somewhat similar circumstances: "Of late you have filled me with so much confidence that I venture to give you some of my thoughts.   My heart is overflowing with love.   First, I admire you for your brains,—I think you have a brilliant mind; secondly, you are a gentle gentleman, and know how to please and treat a lady; thirdly, you are a person one could lean on and feel secure.   But above all you have much good in you.   I believe you love me and that you are true to me." Here we have almost identically the same sentiment that Mary expressed in her portraiture of Bothwell.   If history often repeats itself, love invariably does.

Nor does even John Hosack, Mary's advocate (i. 155), fall short of this testimony.   "Bothwell was the only one of the great nobles of Scotland who from first to last had remained faithful both to her [Mary's] mother and herself. . . . Whatever may have been his follies or his crimes, *no man could say that James Hepburn was either a hypocrite or a traitor.*   Though staunch to the *religion* which he professed, *he never made it the cloak for his ambition;* though driven into exile and reduced to extreme poverty by the malice of his enemies, *he never,* so far as we know, *accepted of a foreign bribe.*   [All the others were for sale or bought.]   In an age when political fidelity was the rarest of virtues, we need not be surprised that his sovereign at this time trusted and rewarded him. . . . Although the common people admired his liberality and courage [his characteristic daring, i. 158] Bothwell among his brother nobles had no friends."   Why?   They envied his gifts and they envied his influence with the Queen.   Need any man ask a higher eulogy than this?

And yet amid all this brutality in manners and mode of living there are glimpses of the influence of gentler natures, which are the more striking from their contrast to the general tone of thought. Witness the following love-letter of Perkin Warbeck to his betrothed, Lady Catharine Gordon, in 1492, the very year in which Columbus discovered America. It is worthy of any person or any period:

> "Most noble lady, it is not without reason that all turn their eyes to you; that all admire, love, and obey you. For they see your two-fold virtues by which you are so much distinguished above all other mortals. Whilst on the one hand they admire your riches and immutable prosperity, which secure to you the nobility of your lineage and the loftiness of your rank, they are, on the other hand, struck by your rather divine than human beauty, and believe that you are not born in our days but descended from heaven.
>
> "All look at your face, so bright and serene that it gives splendour to the cloudy sky; all look at your eyes, as brilliant as stars, which make all pain to be forgotten and turn despair into delight; all look at your neck, which outshines pearls; all look at your fine forehead, your purple light of youth, your fair hair in one word, at the splendid perfection of your person; and looking at, they cannot choose but admire you; admiring, they cannot choose but love you; loving, they cannot choose but obey you.
>
> "I shall perhaps be the happiest of all your admirers and the happiest man on earth, since I have reason to hope you will think me worthy of your love. If I represent to my mind all your perfections I am not only compelled to love but to and to worship you, but love makes me your slave. Whether waking or sleeping, I cannot find rest or happiness except in your affection. All my hopes rest in you, and in you alone.
>
> "Most noble lady, my soul, look mercifully down upon me, your slave, who has ever been devoted to you from the first hour he saw you. Love is not an earthly thing; it is heaven-born. Do not think it below yourself to obey love's dictates. Not only kings but also gods and goddesses have bent their necks beneath its yoke.
>
> "I beseech you, most noble lady, to accept forever one who in all things will cheerfully do your will as long as his days shall last. Farewell, my soul and my consolation. You, the brightest ornament of Scotland, farewell, farewell."

Among those who read at all the minority is very small who have not heard or read of Mary Stuart, Queen of Scots. Of the majority who know something of or sympathize with her, few recall anything of Bothwell but his association with the murder[*] of her miserably vile, hobbledehoy husband, Darnley, and yet how justly does Burton

---

[*] Of these—(the 'Bond against Darnley')—Bothwell was the most formidable. Without any pretence to personal religion he was nominally a Protestant, and therefore obnoxious to the people on the score of Popery. Since his recall from France he had done good service to the Queen, and had risen high in her favor. He was Warden of the Three Marches, Lord High Admiral of Scotland and General of the land forces; and his connections were extensive and powerful. He was held in great dislike by the emissaries of Elizabeth, who had ever found him incorruptible, and he was regarded by the conspirators as the formidable enemy of their schemes. But with all this he was a profligate man of a daring and ambitious spirit, unrestrained by real principle, and ready to go at any lengths for the gratification of his own desires. He was also exceedingly vain; and the preference which was shown him by the Queen, on account of his undoubted services, appears to have awakened hopes which possibly at no earlier period he had entertained."—Aytoun's "Bothwell," 212–13.

observe (iv. 273): "With all her beauty and wit, her political ability and her countless fascinations, Mary, Queen of Scots, would not have occupied nearly the half of her present place in the interest of mankind had the episode of Bothwell not belonged to her story."

The misrepresentations in regard to Bothwell's personal appearance are not more opposite than those in regard to his qualifications and characteristics. Many people might regard this as extremely strange and unaccountable. It is not within a century that Western Europe beheld the apparition of Russia's greatest general. Scarcely any two accounts agree in regard to him, except as to the results that followed his appearance on the different theatres of war. The writer has in his possession works presenting portraits, physical and mental, totally irreconcilable. If Lord Minto, who came in contact intimately with him in Vienna, is correct, all the other accounts to his advantage are miserable flatteries. The writer believes that he was a hero, a genius, but at the same time an eccentric, to such a degree that very often his eccentricity verged on madness, presenting the living exemplification of Dryden's famous lines,—

> " Great wits are sure to madness near allied,
> And thin partitions do their bounds divide."

Or, as Pope phrases it,—

> " What thin partitions sense from thought divide."

About the very time that Suwarrow had risen to distinction, the great New York loyalist, Sir John Johnson, was making himself known and felt. The controversies about Suwarrow's physique and character are about as divergent as the opinions in regard to Sir John held by the Whigs or rebels and the Tories or loyalists. How hard he struck is not susceptible of question, but whether from principle or from vengeance the judgment of men is as wide apart as the poles. History is just as fallible as to the majority of the men who have influenced human progress, as Froude (ix. 321) justly remarks in regard to the Duke of Alva: "The exterminators of the Canaanites are enshrined among the saints, and had the [Roman] Catholics come off victorious [in the Netherlands], the Duke of Alva would have been a second Joshua."

Hough, in his "Northern Invasion" of this State in 1780, has a note on this subject, which applies to every similar case. The gist of it is this: The opinions of local populations in regard to prominent men were entirely biased, if not founded upon their popularity or the reverse. If modern times were to judge of the character of Hannibal by the pictures handed down by the gravest of Roman historians, he would have to be regarded as a man destitute of almost every redeeming trait except courage and ability or astuteness; whereas, when the truth is sifted out, it is positively certain that the very vices attributed to the great Carthaginian should be transferred to his Latin adversaries.

These remarks are most apposite to the case of Bothwell. The great historical Scottish authority of the period of Mary is Buchanan. Burton, the recent exhaustive historian of Scotland (iii. 101, 102 (3), observes: "Great part of his history is fabulous, and when he comes to the controversies in which he took part he was too strong a partisan to be impartial." When it suited his purpose he was a sycophant; when it was to his interest he was a shameless liar. He speaks of Bothwell as looking like an ape in magnificent attire, which leads honest Burton to remark that this "is no more to be taken as accurate than any other scolding objurgation."

All the misrepresentations of Bothwell were in the same spirit as Hogarth's conceptions of Frenchmen, or as the caricatures of Bonaparte during England's fiercest antagonism to her most bitter enemy. Flattery painted the portraits of Mary; envy, hatred, jealousy, and vindictiveness those of Bothwell.

"It is difficult," observes Gibbon (ii. 130), "to form a just idea of his [Clodius Albinus'] true character. Under the philosophic cloak of austerity, he stands accused of concealing most of the vices which degrade human nature. But his accusers are those *venal writers* [as Shakspeare in regard to Richard III., in favor of Henry VII., grandfather of Elizabeth] who adored the fortune of Severus, and trampled on the ashes of an unsuccessful rival."

Brantôme is equally abusive. Burton again meets this with the commentary that Brantôme *may* have met Bothwell, but his language implies that he had *not*. There is proof positive and corroborative that both the Scottish narrator and the French chronicler have falsified the truth. In the first place we have the direct testimony of Gilbert Stuart, who was a passionate partisan, "one of the *most* zealous advocates" of Mary. He paints anything but a disagreeable pen-portrait. "He [Bothwell] was in the prime of youth and extremely handsome." This was when Mary first favored him. Throckmorton, the English envoy, who is no friend to the earl, reported of him, "He is a glorious, rash, and hazardous young man." He writes in Latin, and Bothwell's enemies insinuate that he meant by *gloriosus* something derogatory. Out upon such casuistry! The primal definition of the word is glorious, renowned. According to Littleton it means illustrious,—*illustris, magnificus, praepotens*, PRÆCLARUS. Cicero uses it in the best sense.

Amid all the obloquy that has been heaped upon the mighty Earl, the fact remains unshakable that he was a power that "overtopped" the powerful around him. He was acclimated to broil and battle; as Saul said of Goliath, "he [had been] a man of war from his youth," nay, boyhood, for he had "worn steel since he was twelve years old."

He could "drain a deeper cup, back a wilder horse, ride it like a whirlwind, and couch a heavier spear than the rudest of his jackmen" (Borderers or Moss-troopers); possessed a fine stalwart person, divested of superfluous flesh, "built more like a tower than a man," great strength and military bearing, exercising a fascination over his savage hereditary liegemen that won while it controlled them. His features were manly, bronzed by exposure to the changing vicissitudes of his rough native climate, and his determined mouth was concealed beneath long, drooping moustachios that mingled with his fair curling beard. No wonder that Mary looked upon him with favor, for she had agreeable recollections of his respectful homage when she first wore the white robes of queenly widowhood; and after she returned to Scotland she still found his loyalty so lofty and unchangeable that "it seemed to partake of that devotion which shed a halo over the days of chivalry."

One of the epithets hurled at him by those who hated and feared him is the stigma that he was "one-eyed." But the same designation is applicable to Hannibal, perhaps the greatest individual not a king who ever trod the earth, and to Potemkin, the mighty Russian Potentate, who never lost the heart of the Empress Catherine II., nor his control of herself and her empire. If, however, the Earl had lost the sight of an eye in combat, by sea or land, the orb itself was uninjured, and it has been observed that the scar on his forehead, which was the only visible vestige of the injury, "became his face as it would have become none other." Men are not always disfigured by such casualties; and it is well known that Marie Louise, daughter of imperial Austria, willingly exchanged the embraces of the Emperor Napoleon for those of Count Niepper, an extraordinarily handsome Austrian officer, although he had actually lost an eye in battle and wore a patch or bandage.

Bothwell, like Mary, was entirely out of the common. His appearance was no index to his age. He was one of those so completely imbued with vitality that years pass over them and leave none of the traces which stamp, season after season, their impress on ordinary men, or scar them deeply, as the glaciers furrow the rocks over which they glide, grinding on age by age, leaving channels that remain indelible after the superincumbent ice has melted away. There may have been silver mingled with his darker locks, but this was not the result of time but of thought, just as in the days of plate-armor a soldier could be recognized by fringes of gray where the helmet had pressed most closely and persistently, while everywhere else the original color held its own. He was a curious commingling of the self-possession that results from deep thought and severe discipline of mind and body in war, politics, and courts and the mobility which is inseparable from an original nervous temperament while as yet the frame has not known sufficient rest to take on superfluous flesh. If Michael Angelo's *Penseroso*—Guiliano, NOT Lorenzo de Medici—could have been transmitted from bronze into flesh, effigy would have lived in such a man as Bothwell.

It is as difficult to decide what constitutes the handsome in man as in woman. Figure has as much to do with it as face, but whenever the latter indicates mind and manliness and is susceptible of illumination from within it cannot be otherwise than handsome. It matters not the color of the eye for effect, in the excitement of passion the light eye often becomes dark, and there are hazel eyes which when they scintillate or burn, have no color, they are simply living fires,—diamonds of the clearest and intensest lustre.

Contemporaries attributed the domination exercised by Bothwell over Mary to necromancy; but the best answer to such a charge is that made by the unfortunate Leonora Galigai,—daughter of the nurse of Mary de Medicis, and widow of the assassinated Concino Concini, Marshal d'Ancre,—when accused of similar powers over the Florentine queen of Henry IV. of France. She replied, " My arts were simply the superiority of a strong mind over a weak one." As regarded Bothwell Mary Stuart was weak, however strong in other cases. While so many writers have sought to degrade and even to caricature Bothwell, there are some who seek to do him justice without the slightest sacrifice of truth.

Bothwell was a gentleman of ancient race. He had the manners of a great lord, and the haughtiness of a feudal noble. His resolute features never blushed. His eyes were beautiful, although one had been deprived of vision; but he was far from being disfigured by the accident. Indeed, the defect of his sight was hardly perceptible. His voice, which had a genuine manly ring, was susceptible of the gentlest inflections. His mouth expressed his feeling of superiority. He had a marked nose and a patrician physiognomy, and his fascinating look resembled that of an eagle. This martial visage, this noble and easy figure, this soul without scruples, this mind full of audacity and ambition, carried the queen away. To this must be added the attest of Sir Walter Scott as to " the bold address and courtly manners of Bothwell," " a nobleman possessed of his great power and hereditary influence."

" All these [his] ' gifts of hell' were relieved by a lofty demeanor and by an air that seemed to defy fortune, danger, and adversity." Alas ! Whence came " these gifts of Hell?" In all things Bothwell was more sinned against than sinning, according to the touchstone of humanity and the measuring-rod of his times. It is said that Bothwell was in love with Mary from the first moment that he beheld his " *Reine Blanche*" in the Park of Fontainebleau, as early as 1560, and that he welcomed her home with a loyalty as pure as his devotion was strong. His captivity in Edinburgh Castle by the warrant of Mary, to gratify Murray and his party, is said to have changed the whole nature of Bothwell. He felt that he had suffered a grievous injustice from one to whom he had given heart and hand, or, rather, brand; and after his release he brooded over the wrong until his naturally violent temper overcame all gentler restraints. His temper had hitherto resembled a mountain lake, confined within bounds by artificial barriers. Thus dyked it fed a swift and ever-beneficent stream, but as soon as storm and flood had breached the bulwark it poured forth a wild and unrestrainable torrent that wasted where it had formerly blessed. Mary was Scotch stock, developed by French cultivation; Bothwell, a Scotch-barbaric-aristocratic scion, refined by French influence and association. Both were congenial in origin and identical in seed. Like was drawn to like; they mutually attracted each other. Bothwell was brave to a degree sufficient to encounter any peril. Still, it is true that, while he possessed the physical courage which triumphs triumphantly and succumbs without yielding, his end did not manifest the purest, the highest moral intrepidity inspired by fanaticism or love. If he had possessed either of these grander forms of courage he could not have been induced to abandon the field at Carberry Hill without one desperate blow stricken for the trusting woman who loved him so intensely as to sacrifice everything for him. Nor would he have lingered out so many years in captivity. The real bird of prey would have beaten out its life against the bars of its prison, or soon would have drooped and died in captivity. . . .

What is the reality of the pen-portrait of Bothwell, drawn and colored by the enmity of Murray's panegyric? Bothwell was handsome, smart, alluring, fearless, utterly free from the superstitions and fanaticism of his era; ambitious, a lay Richelieu, who, when he saw his *objective*, reached it by clearing away obstacles. He was not as politic or self-restrained as Moray, or Murray, but he was far more trustworthy. In every respect he was as far superior to the avaricious and dissolute Morton, to the unprincipled Huntley, and to the combined or simple vices inherent in the rest of the prominent Scottish nobility as he may have failed in the feigned decorum of the regent, in whom the shrewd instincts of the fox were in complete ascendency over those of the wolf. For his generation Bothwell was not as bad as many men whose opportunities for evil were not in accordance with their vile desires. Not to be absolutely vicious where the many,—with rare exceptions,—were altogether so, entitles him to a consideration and a fair judgment which is inconsistent with the influences of to-day. Circumstances alone make men, and men must be judged by the circumstances which environed and mastered them. Many a man and many a woman who pass for saints in the nineteenth century might have been very devils had they lived in Scotland or in France three hundred and twenty-five years ago.

Bothwell's religious convictions were directly opposite to those of Mary. He was a Protestant. Such a combination of principle and the want of it in a man stigmatized by his enemies as very wicked may be a seeming paradox, but it is not unexampled. Many a man who appears to be destitute of principle possesses, nevertheless, underlying everything, a determination in regard to doctrine which is inaccessible to force, to bribe, or to seduction,—a bed-rock belief which defies fire itself. Everything seemed calculated to separate the bigoted Papist, Mary, and the unyielding Presbyterian, Bothwell. It appeared, however, as if even the vices of so strange a lover, their mutual divergences, united to make him irresistible in the heart of the queen, corrupted in its first developing bud in the flagitious Court of the Valois, in which the presiding Circe was Catherine de Medicis, surrounded by her one hundred and fifty *filles d'honneur* (*sic*), the sirens of her Italian policy. Mary and Bothwell *were* physical, moral, and mental enigmas while living, and they *are* still enigmas.

Scarcely three months elapsed after the murder of Darnley before Mary was remarried to Bothwell, and the funeral baked meats

" Did coldly furnish forth the marriage table,"

not merely poetically. This may seem horrible, and, indeed, it would be so under ordinary circumstances. And yet the apparently inexplicable may be made comprehensible by a careful consideration of the occurrences. The life of Mary hitherto had been rather one of positive suffering than of relative happiness. The miserably sickly husband of her youth and superb blossoming had died after nineteen months of a prolonged exhaustive honeymoon, throughout which the wife had been little better than a nurse or governess. The interval between the death of Francis and the espousal with Darnley was certainly one of trial of heart, mind, and even body. Mary expected to find in her again young husband a solace and a support. He proved to be neither. His youthful vigor, his fine person, and good looks were masks that concealed a vile disposition and an insane ambition ; and his efforts to obtain the crown-matrimonial, with an authority equal, if not superior, to that of Mary, were characterized by exhibitions and efforts that prove him to have been devoid of any manliness, and of every other quality which might have measurably redeemed his base ingratitude and his want of intelligence. He assassinated the queen's affection for him, aroused and stimulated by his outside attractions, almost as suddenly by not only planning but assisting in the dastardly murder of the unhappy Rizzio. Mary, who to feminine graces united masculine courage and energy, saw in Bothwell the qualities which constitute a " REAL MAN." He had befriended her, sustained her, championed

3

her; he was fearless, devoted; in short, a rough but resolute Scottish lord, and also a bold Scottish MAN, far better and in no wise worse than his peers in rank,—yes, better than all in one quality or another, even than Murray. Mary's best affections had been crushed in upon herself by the adverse circumstances of her position and the meannesses of her husband. They had been chilled by an utter absence of the sympathy, in all around her save in Bothwell, which she so greatly needed,—a sympathy necessary to bring out and develop all that was loving and lovable in her nature. When freed from such a mate as Darnley, her affections, suddenly relieved from the terrible pressure of the ties that bound her, her very capability of feeling, stretched itself out, as a vine planted in the darkness of a vault grows towards the crevices through which filters a single ray of light; and then, when her arms thus expanded to the warmth and comfort and confidence of a new hope, a new faith, a new love, when her arms and hands, outstretched beseechingly, met each other again in a fond embrace,—those beautiful, soft, white, rounded arms, and the hands that betrayed her at Lochleven Castle,—they enclosed—Bothwell!

Or when, crushed in her affections and her spirits, she opened wide her arms for sympathy, support, and love, and the expanded fingers, which were symmetry itself, drew together and clasped each other again about the columnar support she so greatly needed, and for which she yearned, they locked within the magic circle of that yearning quest the hero of her dreams, the stalwart Bothwell!

    *   *   *   *   *   *   *   *

So far for actual proof as to the traits and attractiveness of Bothwell. Now as to the corroborative evidence. When, in 1562, through the temporary ascendency and enmity of Murray, Bothwell fled to France, the king, Charles IX., appointed him one of his chamberlains. The House of Valois liked to have handsome men and women around them. Is it likely that Charles IX. would have selected a foreigner repulsively ugly, without grace and accomplishments, to be near his person? The supposition is supremely ridiculous, and this fact alone gives the lie both to Buchanan and Brantôme. When, again, in 1563, the malice of his enemies drove Bothwell forth he again repaired to the Court of France, and Charles IX. made him Commander of his Scots Guard, to whom was intrusted the protection of his person. In the "Scot Abroad" Burton discourses as follows:

"The SCOTS GUARD consisted of one hundred *gens d'armes* and two hundred archers. They had a Captain who was a High Officer of State. The first Captain of the Guard who appears in history—and probably the first person who held the office—was John Stewart, Lord of Aubigne, the founder of a great Scots House in France. . . . By a chivalrous courtesy the appointment to this high office was confided to the King of Scots. This was an arrangement, however, that could not last. As the two nations changed their relative positions, and the Guard began to become

Scots only in name, it became not only out of the question that the captain should be appointed by a foreign government, but impolitic that he should be a foreigner. It is curious to notice a small ingenious policy to avoid offense to the haughty foreigners in the removal of the command from the Scots. The first Captain of the Guard who was a native Frenchman was the Count of Montgomery, who, for his patrimonial name, which corresponded with that of an old Scots family, passed for a man of Scots descent. It was thought prudent that his son should succeed him ; but the selection was not fortunate, for he was the same Montgomery who hit [and mortally wounded] King Henry II. at the jousts in honor of his daughter Elizabeth's marriage to Philip II., and so made Mary Stewart, Queen of France.

" According to the old courtly creed of France, the privileges of the Scots Guard had an eminence that partook of sacredness. Twenty-four of them were told off as the special protectors of the royal person. They took charge of the keys of the chamber where the king slept, and the oratory where he paid his devotions. When, on a solemn progress, he entered a walled town, the keys were committed to the custody of the captain of the Guard. They guarded his boat as he crossed a ferry, and were essential to the support of his litter when he was carried. On ordinary occasions two of them stood behind him ; but in affairs of great ceremony—the reception of embassies, the conferring of high honors, the touching for the king's evil, and the like—six of them stood near the throne, three on either side. It was deemed a marked honor to them that the silk fringe with which their halberts were decorated was white, the royal color of France.

" There is something melancholy beyond description in contemplating the condition of a country the vital treasures of which had to be confided to the fidelity and bravery of hireling strangers. If there was a fault in the affair, however, it was not with the Scots : they were true to their trust, and paid faith with faith.

" On their side of the bargain, too, there is something touching in the picture of a hardy, high-spirited race robbed of their proper field of exertion at home, and driven to a foreign land, there to bestow the enterprising energy that might have made their own illustrious, and serving a foreign master with the single-minded fidelity that had been nourished within them by the love of their own land and kindred. But it must be admitted that their hospitable patrons made their exile mighty comfortable. When the lank youth left behind him the house of his ancestors, standing up gray, cold, and bare on the bleak moorland, it was not to pass into hard sordid exile, but rather to exult in the prospect of a land of promise or El Dorado, and faithfully was the promise kept ; for the profuse hospitality and lavish generosity of France to her guests is a thing hardly to be elsewhere paralleled in history. It was but just that it should all be requited with sound fidelity and ardent devotion.

" The trust which Louis XI. reposed in the Guard has been already referred to. It was not their blame that he took their assistance in grubbing up the roots of all the political institutions which checked or modified the supreme authority of the Crown. If we were to suppose, indeed, that they passed beyond the routine of duty to think of the political results of the affairs in which they were engaged, they would find a good many partisans in the present day had they adopted the designs of their crafty master as their own, and backed them as the soundest policy for the future of France and of Europe at large, for Louis XI. is by no means championless.

" In one of the most amusing of all the chronicles ever written—that of Comines—the Scots Guard figure frequently and always creditably. Louis, who was reputed to trust no other creatures of human make, appears to have placed entire reliance on them. They saved him at a crisis of great peril in his renowned attack, along with the Duke of Burgundy, on the city of Liege. Both potentates were deeply plotting, the one to bring the Burgundian territories directly under the Crown of France, the other to change his Dukedom for a Kingdom, which might in the end comprise France itself. Both were of one mind, for the time, in deadly malice and murderous projects against the industrious burghers of the city. By a concurrence of events which broke through the fine texture of his subtle policy, Louis found himself in the hands of his fierce rival, for he was within the lines of Burgundy's army, with no other resource or protection apparently but his Scots Guard. There was to be a storming of Liege, which was to be anticipated by the citizens breaking out and attacking the camp of the Duke. In the confusion of such an affair at such a juncture, it is easy to suppose that Louis could not know friends from enemies, and had reason to believe the enemies to be far the more prevalent of the two. Comines gives this distinct and homely narrative of what he saw of the affair, for he was present:

" ' I, and two gentlemen more of his bed-chamber, lay that night in the Duke of Burgundy's chamber (which was very small), and above us there were twelve archers upon the guard, all of 'em in their clothes, and playing at dice. His main guard was at a good distance, and towards the gate of the town ; in short, the master of the house where the Duke was quartered, having drawn out a good party of the *Liegeois*, came so suddenly upon the Duke he had scarce time to put on his back and breast plate and clap a steel cap upon his head. As soon as he had done it we ran down the stairs into the street; but we found our archers engaged with the enemy, and much ado they had to defend the doors and the windows against 'em.' . . . .'

" The King was also assaulted after the same manner by his landlord, who entered his house, but was slain by the *Scotch* Guard. These *Scotch* troops behaved themselves valiantly, maintained their ground, would not stir one step from the King, and were very nimble with their bows and arrows, with which, it is said, they wounded and killed more of the Burgundians than of the enemy. . . .

" French historians are tolerably unanimous in their testimony that the Guard were faithful fellows. As a small select body of men, highly endowed with rank and remuneration, they were naturally the prize-holders of a considerable body of their countrymen, who in the army of France strove to prove themselves worthy of reception into the chosen band. Thus the Scots in the French army carried the spirit of the service beyond the mere number selected as the Guard ; and there was among them a fellow-feeling mixed with a devotion to the Crown of France, of a kind which there is no good term for in English, while it is but faintly expressed by the French *esprit de corps*. A few of the facts in the history of the Scots troops employed by France bring it closer home than any generalization can ; for instance, after other incidents of a like character, M. Michel quotes from D'Auton's chronicle, how, in a contest with the Spaniards in Calabria, in 1503, the banner-bearer, William Turnbull, was found dead with the staff in his arms and the flag gripped in his teeth, with a little cluster of his countrymen round him, killed at their posts, ' et si un Écossais était mort d'un côté un Espagnol ou deux l'étaient de l'autre.' The moral drawn from this incident by the old chronicler is that the expression long proverbial in France, ' *Fier comme un Écossais,*' was because the Scots ' aimaient mieux mourir pour honneur garder, que vivre en honte, reprochez de tache de lacheté.'

" When the two British kingdoms merged towards each other in the sixteenth century, the native element was gradually turned out of the Scots Guard. When Scotland became part of an empire which called France the natural enemy, it seemed unreasonable that her sons should expect to retain a sort of supremacy in the French army. But there are no bounds to human unreasonableness when profitable offices are coming and going, and many of our countrymen during the seventeenth century were loud in their wrath and lamentation about the abstraction of their national privileges in France. Some Scotchmen, still in the Guard in the year 1611, had a quarrel with the French captain, De Montespan, and brought their complaints before King James. As French soldiers appealing to a foreign monarch, they were very naturally dismissed. Of course they now complained at home still more loudly, and their cause was taken up by some great men. The French behaved in the matter with great courtesy. The men dismissed for a breach of discipline could not be replaced at the instigation of a foreign Court, but the Government would fill their places with other Scotsmen duly recommended. So lately as the year 1642, demands were made on the French Government to renew the ancient League and restore the 'privileges' of the Scots in France, including the monopoly of the appointments in the Guard. But though made in the name of King Charles I. by the Scots Privy Council, these demands were, like many of the other transactions of the day, rather made in hostility to the King than in obedience to his commands. Louis XIV. gave a brief and effective answer to them. He said that he would renew the League only on the condition that the Scots should cease to act as the ally of England, either by giving obedience to the King of that country 'or under pretext of religion, without express permission from the King, their master,'—a pretty accurate diplomatic description of the position of the Covenanting force.

"Down to the time when all the pomps and vanities of the French Crown were swept away along with its substantial power, the Scots Guard existed as pageant of the Court of France. In that immense conglomerate of all kinds of useful and useless knowledge, the 'Dictionnaire de Trevoux,' it is set forth that 'la premiere compagnie des Gardes du Corps de nos rois' is still called 'La Garde Écossaise,' though there was not then (1730) a single Scotsman in it. Still there were preserved among the young Court lackeys, who kept up the part of the survivors of the Hundred Years' War, some of the old formalities. Among these, when the *Clerc du Guêt* challenged the guard who had seen the palace-gate closed, 'il repond en Écossais, "I am hire"—c'est à dire, me voilà;' and the lexicographer informs us that, in the mouths of the Frenchmen, totally unacquainted with the barbarous tongue in which the regimental orders had been originally devised, the answer always sounded, 'Ai am hire.'

"In some luxurious libraries may be found a gorgeous volume in old morocco, heavily decorated with symbols of royalty, bearing on its engraved title-page that it is 'La Sacre de Louis XV. Roy de France et de Navarre, dans l'Eglise de Reims, le Dimanche, xxv Octobre, MDCCXXII.' After a poetical inauguration, giving assurance of the piety, the justice, the firmness, the devotion to his people of the new King, and the orthodoxy, loyalty, and continued peace that were to be the lot of France, with many other predictions wide of the truth that came to pass, there come a series of large pictures, representing the various stages of the coronation, and these are followed by full-dress and full-length portraits of the various high officers who figured on the solemn occasion. Among these we have the Capitaine des Gardes Écossais in full state uniform. This has anything but a military aspect; it is the single-breasted broad-flapped coat of the time, heavily embroidered, a short mantle, and a black cap, with a double white plume. The six guards are also represented in a draped portrait. It is far more picturesque than that of their captain, yet, in its white satin, gold embroidery, and fictitious mail, it conveys much less of the character of the soldier than that of the court attendant. . . . In the original engraving, by the way, the artist has thrown an air of absorbed devotedness into the very handsome countenance drawn by him, which is at variance, in some measure, with the tone of the attitude and costume, as pertaining to a mere figure in a state pageant."

Is it consistent with the remotest bounds of human perversity, not born of absolute personal hatred and unprincipled malice, to imagine for a moment that so great a king as the monarch of France, at a time when his realm was convulsed with civil and religious antagonism, when questions of state and feeling were riddles to be solved by steel, poison, or prostitution, would have conferred one of the grandest charges of the crown—the care of his person, the guardianship of his privacy—to a foreigner if that stranger had not possessed the highest

reputation for courage and fidelity at home, for loyalty tried and un-
stained by doubt, noble in appearance, equally noble in character, brave
as the steel with which he had to guard and protect, and as strong in
physical strength as determined in will and devotion?   The very
attempt to caricature Bothwell in the light of the dignities to which he
rose shows a petty malice which, if it were to be met with among libel-
ers to-day, would inevitably awaken the conviction that a writer guilty
of such scurrility was not worthy even the notice of a kicking.

What were the antecedents of this Bothwell?   When James III.
of Scotland lowered himself, according to the ideas of the aristocracy,
to an association with plebeians or mechanics, the nobility asserted the
rights they considered inherent in their class by hanging the king's
favorites on the Bridge of Lauder, all but one, a youth of seventeen
named Ramsay.   He was spared in answer to the entreaties of his
master, who created him Lord or Earl of Bothwell.   Even Dr. Petrick, *our* Bothwell's great defender, falls into the gross error of arguing
that the nobility in 1540–67 hated the Bothwell who married Mary
because he was descended from this plebeian Ramsay.   James III.
desired to bestow with the title the lordship of Bothwell upon Ramsay, but it "was not to be had, because it was in the fast grip of the
Hepburns,"—an ancient race, these Hepburns of Hales.   Although
this young royal favorite was made titular Lord Bothwell about 1482,
his royal master did not live long enough to establish him.   The con-
federated nobility took up arms against their detested king in 1488,
and defeated him at Sauchie-burn, 11th June of that year, near the
famous Bannockburn battle-field, where THE Bruce won independence
for Scotland, 25th June, 1314.   Flying from the field, James III. was
murdered at Beaton's Mill, on the east side of the Bannockburn, and
his son James IV. succeeded.   He created Lord Patrick Hepburn
Earl of Bothwell, and bestowed upon him the hereditary office of Lord
High Admiral of Scotland, along with many other dignities and extensive possessions.   His son Adam, the second Earl, fell by the side
of his king, James IV., in the Battle of Flodden, so fatal to the Scottish nobility.   Sir Walter Scott commemorates his death in his poem of
Marmion, Canto IV., ¶ xii.:

> " Another aspect Crichtoun showed,
>   As through its portals Marmion rode;
>   But yet 'twas melancholy state
>   Received him at the outer gate;
>   For none were in the Castle then
>   But women, boys, or aged men.
>   With eyes scarce dried, the sorrowing dame
>   To welcome noble Marmion came;
>   Her son, a stripling twelve years old,
>   Proffer'd the Baron's rein to hold;
>   For each man that could draw a sword
>   Had march'd that morning with their lord,

> Earl ADAM HEPBURN, he who died
> On Flodden, by his sovereign's side.
> Long may his Lady look in vain:
> She ne'er shall see his gallant train
> Come sweeping back through Crichtoun Dean.
> 'Twas a brave race before the name
> Of hated Bothwell stained their fame."

It may be interesting to know how Crichtoun Castle came into the hands of the Hepburns. Lord Crichtoun, its previous owner, had seduced the Princess Margaret, sister to James III., out of revenge, it is said, because that Monarch had dishonored Crichtoun's own wife. The king, furious at this method of retaliation, this fair application of the *lex talionis*, besieged and took the Castle, and transferred it to the Hepburns.

This Adam Bothwell distinguished himself greatly by a furious attempt, with the reserve, to retrieve the defeat at Flodden, as is celebrated in an old poem, "Flodden Field," edited by H. Weber, Edinburgh, 1804:

> "Then on the Scottish part, right proud,
> The Earl of Bothwell then out brast,
> And stepping forth, with stomach good
> Into the enemies' throng he thrust;
> And *Bothwell! Bothwell!* cried bold,
> To cause his soldiers to ensue;
> But there he caught a welcome cold,—
> The Englishmen straight down him threw.
> Thus Haburn through his hardy heart
> His fatal fine in conflict found."

Patrick, third Earl of Bothwell, was still a minor when his father, Adam, fell beside his king at Flodden. It is very curious, but none of the Bothwells lived long enough to see their children attain to majority. This third Earl, Patrick, was known to his countrymen as "the Fair Earl." The English, who found in him, as in his son afterwards, a patriotic antagonist to their schemes, defamed him, as they subsequently did his son. Sadler, the British representative, considered him "the most vain and insolent man in the world, full of pride and folly," or else "the proudest and haughtiest man in all Scotland." Evidently the English could not bend to their purposes or buy the honor of the third any more than the fourth Earl Bothwell. Hence their venom. In 1535, Patrick married Agnes Sinclair. She belonged to a family of Norman origin, and one of the most renowned in Scotland as well as on the continent of Europe. This Agnes, "the Lady of Morham," was the mother of a daughter, Jane, and a son, James, THE Bothwell of scandal, history, and romance. In 1543 she was divorced from her husband, who died three years after, in 1556. James, her son, never forfeited her affections, and she was his good angel as long as her influence could benefit him, that is, until he was finally driven from Scotland. She died in 1573. The divorce did not result from any wrong-doing on her part. There is little doubt that Earl Patrick took advantage of a plea which was a fertile cause of divorces as long as the Pope and Romanist priests had any power in his native country,—the plea of consanguinity. The real cause, no doubt, lay in the hopes entertained by Earl Patrick that, if he was free to marry, he could obtain the hand of Mary of Guise, widow of James V., Queen Dowager and Regent of Scotland. Thus he expected to become the real head and power and the source of honor in Scotland. He was justified in his expectation, since twice in writing the Queen Regent promised faithfully to marry him. Why she did not actually give her hand to the Fair Earl is susceptible of several explanations. Rumor insinuated that she was overfond of the Primate, Cardinal Beaton. His cloth forbade the idea of a legal tie. While this consideration was pending, Earl Patrick died. James V. died in 1542, Earl Bothwell was divorced in 1543, and died in 1556, and Mary, the Regent, expired 10th June, 1560. The strange doings of " the fair Earl," Patrick, whose ways were often dark and tricks vain, cast a black shadow over the career of his son, the heir to his titles, properties, and dignities. It is admitted by all fair critics that the two have been often confounded to the detriment of the latter. The father's evil reputation was in some respects an almost fatal injury to the son.

In aspiring to the hand of the famous Mary, James Hepburn, Earl of Bothwell, the subject of this article, was simply obeying the traditions of his house, and taking advantage of his qualifications and position. When Mary's first husband, Francis II., died, Bothwell was the trusted, tried, almost single true-hearted supporter of her mother and the latter's agent in France. It is true that the hand of the young widow was sought by princes and the sons of kings, but among the suitors proposed and proposing were nobles strongly pressed who were not as eminent as Bothwell. Finally the list of the eligible was reduced to two ; Dudley, a younger son, the choice of Elizabeth and her darling, who was not created Earl of Leicester until this contemplated elevation was quite advanced, and Darnley, who was of no account and without influence until he was promoted to an Earldom, which was not done until about a month after he had been " handfasted" to Mary. Bothwell was born the most richly endowed and powerful nobleman, except Lord Hamilton, in Scotland, with the greatest number of vassals in that southern portion of the kingdom, a belted Earl and Lord High Admiral of the Realm, Sheriff of three counties, Bailiff or Queen's representative in another. When he was certainly not over twenty-eight years of age he was Lieutenant-General under the Crown, and virtually Commander-in-Chief of the Scottish army in the field. What is more, he sat in Parliament before he was of age, and was Lieutenant-General, or Warden of the

Borders, as soon as he attained his majority, and Queen's Commissioner, or Representative, to guard the interests of the Crown and his country, in opposition to the English agents (one the Duke of Bedford), before Darnley made his appearance. Finally, not to spin out the story, he was Captain of the French Scots, or Royal, Guard, in his twenty-seventh year. If this does not prove manliness and character, what will suffice to satisfy opinion on such subjects?

What is more and more to the point, the Hepburns had always aimed high. A Hepburn of Bothwell married a sister of the great Robert Bruce, the victor of Bannockburn and deliverer of Scotland in 1290. The grandfather of the first Earl, Patrick, of Hales, held very curious relations in regard to the beautiful Jane Beaufort, widow of James I., who died in 1436. This Lord Patrick Hepburn, of Hales, was master of the famous Castle of Dunbar, and there, with him, the lovely Jane spent her latter days and died. History has never solved the riddle of the ties that united them. Adam, son of this Lord Patrick, was among the many lovers of Mary of Gueldres, widow of James II., deceased in 1460. Is it very extraordinary that James Hepburn should not forget the good fortune of his great-great-great-grandfather and of his great-great-grandfather when they were simple Lords and not mighty Earls, and of his father, the third great "belted" Earl? When and where—after he was old enough to experience the power of love—he first saw Queen Mary does not appear. But this fact is well known, he was very high in the favor of her mother when, early in 1561, at Joinville, in France, shortly after the death of her royal husband, he did wait upon the peerless "La Reine Blanche," to whom, according to the poets, even the trees and rocks bowed and did obeisance as she walked through the forest and glades of Fontainebleau, or, as Ronsard sang:

> " The ivory whiteness of thy bosom fair;
> The long and slender hand, so soft and rare;
> Thy all-surpassing look and form of love,
> Enchanting as a vision from above;
> Then thy sweet voice and music of thy speech,
> That rocks and woods might move, nor art could reach,—
> When these are lost, fled to a foreign shore,
> With loves and graces France beholds no more,
> How shall the poet sing now thou art gone?
> For silent is the muse since thou hast flown.
> All that is beauteous short time doth abide;
> The rose and lily only bloom while lasteth the springtide.

> " Thus here, in France, thy beauty only shone
> For thrice five years, and suddenly is gone;
> Like to the lightning-flash, a moment bright,
> To leave but darkness and regret like night,
> To leave a deathless memory behind,
> Of that fair princess, in my heart enshrined.

4

My winged thoughts, like birds, now fly to thee,
My beauteous princess, and her home I see,
And there for evermore I fain would stay,
Nor from that sweetest dwelling ever stray.

"Nature hath ever, in her deepest floods,
On loftiest hills, in lonely rocks and woods,
Her choicest treasures hid from mortal ken,
With rich and precious gems unseen of men.
The pearl and ruby sleep in secret stores,
And softest perfumes spring on wildest shores.
Thus God, who over thee his watch doth keep,
Hath borne thy beauty safe across the deep
On foreign shore, in regal pride to rest,
Far from mine eyes, but hidden in my breast."

One of the most extraordinary and unaccountable facts connected with the history of Mary Stuart is the contradictory and irreconcilable evidence in regard to her personal appearance.[5] The only likeness which is known to be authentic is that recognized as " the famous Sheffield portrait," preserved in Hardwick Hall and belonging to the Duke of Devonshire.   It represents the Queen in her thirty-sixth year, as

[5] " As there are ill-fated persons, there are also ill-fated families. The fortunes of Mary are but one scene in the long and fearful *Tragedy of the Stuarts.* Her ancestor in the sixth degree upwards, King Robert III., had a nephew named *Alexander Stuart, who, at the beginning of the fifteenth century, murdered Malcolm Drummond, the brother of the Queen of Scotland, and married his widow Isabella, with her consent,—a counterpart or antitype of the history of Darnley, Bothwell, and Mary.* The Duke of Albany, brother of King Robert, threw his son and his own nephew Rothsay into prison, and let him starve till he gnawed the flesh off his own limbs, and then died. As soon as Rothsay's brother, James I., the father of Mary's great-great-grandfather, ascended the throne, he sought and found an opportunity to have all the sons of the Duke of Albany beheaded, for which, in the year 1436, and partly by his own relations, he was attacked and killed with sixteen wounds. James's widow sacrificed the perpetrators to the manes of her husband in a manner which calls to mind the vengeance of Queen Agnes for King Albert of Germany. James II., Mary's great-great-grandfather, caused two of his cousins, the Douglasses, to be beheaded, murdered the third with his own hands, and perished by a violent death at the siege of Roxburgh. His son, James III., Mary's great-grandfather, was engaged in a sanguinary contest, first with his brother, the Duke of Albany, and then with his own son. He lost, against the latter, the battle of Sauchieburn, and was assassinated on his flight. James IV., Mary's grandfather, did not enjoy the happiness which he expected in the sovereignty that he had unjustly acquired, and was killed in the battle of Floddenfield. James V., Mary's father, lost his senses through grief at the disobedience of the nobility and the failure of his plans, and died eight days after the birth of his daughter.

" Such were the ancestors of Mary ! and now her descendants : James I. (VI.), Charles I., Charles II., and James II., four kings of whom it is difficult to say whether they were more unfortunate or more unworthy. Before the Stuarts lost their power for the second time and forever, James II. caused his nephew, the Duke of Monmouth, to be executed, and thus concluded the three hundred years' series of bloody deeds and fortunes of this ill-fated race !"—" *Contributions to Modern History, from the British Museum and the State Paper Office, known as Queen Elizabeth and Queen Mary.*" By Frederick von Raumer, London, 1836, p. 430-2.

an extremely tall, long-faced, long-nosed, long-limbed, long-fingered woman, with a very decided cast in the right eye. Her mother was a woman of heroic proportions, and Mary must have towered as well, for in a picture of herself and Darnley, who was known as a "well-made, long lad," she equals her husband in height. The beautiful picture which is accepted as a trustworthy portrait of Mary, was "*constructed to satisfy his ideal*," on the order of her biographer, Chalmers, by Mr. Pailou, "a very ingenious artist," who took the picture, owned by the Earl of Morton, as the basis of his work, which (the original) was burned with the Castle of Alloa, in which it had been preserved, in 1800.

"The painter," says Dr. Stoddart, who saw this picture a few months before its destruction, "was no mean artist; and the piece, though hard, was highly finished. The features were probably drawn with accuracy, but *what little character they possessed was unpleasant, and might better have suited the cold and artful Elizabeth* than the tender, animated Mary. It appeared, however, to have been painted at an age when she had been long written 'in sour Misfortune's book;' and had perhaps lost that warmth of feeling which was at once the bane of her happiness and the charm of her manners."

The color of Mary's eyes varies—according to different writers— from the blue or gray, which are not distinguishable, to dark brown, and the hue of her hair from a flaxen inclining to red, through every intermediate shade, to dark brown or black. The writer possesses or has seen over a hundred portraits, and no two are alike. In one taken in France at the time of her marriage with the Dauphin she has reddish-yellow hair and light eyes, and in the "Hardwick portrait," painted at the close of her life, she has small, very dark, cunning eyes, a foxy nose, and black or dark brown hair. It is more than probable that if she had not been a Queen she would not have attracted notice by her looks.

How, then, has the almost universal mistake occurred in regard to her personal attractiveness? Bell, perhaps, explains it (Life of Mary, i. 74). There was a noblewoman, "a celebrated Continental beauty, a Countess of Mansfeldt," prominent at the Court of France during the life of Mary, who, it was claimed, bore a striking resemblance to the Scottish Queen. Portraits of this lady were multiplied and dispersed throughout Europe, and *these*—not originals from life—are the likenesses which have been accepted as correct presentations of the unfortunate Mary Stuart.

Before dismissing this consideration, which results in the conviction that Mary's transcendent beauty is a myth, it may satisfy the credulous to know that in Dalkeith Castle, "the principal residence of the noble (*sic*) family of Morton," there was another authentic (?) portrait of the Queen. Of this Gilpin, the tourist or traveler, writes thus: "Here, and in almost all the great houses of Scotland, we have pictures of

Queen Mary; but their authenticity is often doubted from the circumstance of her hair. In one it is auburn, in another black, and in another yellow. Notwithstanding, however, this difference, it is very possible that all these pictures may be genuine. [How can this possibly be?] We have a letter preserved, from Mr. White, a servant of Queen Elizabeth, to Sir William Cecil, in which he mentions his having seen Queen Mary at Tutbury Castle. ‘She is a goodly personage,’ says he, ‘hath an *alluring grace,* a pretty Scottish speech, a searching wit, and great mildness. Her hair of itself is black; but Mr. Knolls told me that *she wears hair of sundry colors.’”*

That Mary was fascinating in an almost inconceivable degree, highly educated and accomplished, endowed with a brilliant and active mind, "*mens sana in corpore sano,*" there can be no doubt, and her epistolary style has been greatly eulogized. Bothwell, by several styled almost illiterate, wrote much better than she did, and yet no one ever extolled his compositions. She has been styled a poet; she did write pretty verses it is true; but not better than hundreds who furnish contributions to magazines at a stipulated price per page, and even her famous lines on quitting France are said to have been written subsequently for her by a better "maker,"—*i.e.*, real poet.

The fact is she was an accomplished coquette and permeated with electrifying feline fascination, and she was a crowned head. The title put the seal to the whole. Endowed with natural graces, enhanced by her sojourn in the most polished court of Europe, she must have appeared like a phenomenon amid the brutal beauties of Scotland, and as a living light amid "the darkness which could be felt" of the manners and morals of the Scottish nobility of a savage and uncultured period. As a Woman, in the presence-chamber or a ball-room she was enchanting, and as a Queen, the mode and the rage, an Enchantress.

"Can a queen ever know whether it is her face or her diadem that is loved? That rays of her starry crown dazzle the eyes and the heart. . . . A queen is something so far removed from men, so elevated, so widely separated from them, so impossible for them to reach! What presumption dare flatter itself in such an enterprise? It is not simply a woman, it is an august and sacred being that has no sex, and that is worshipped kneeling without being loved."

Mary was a Circe, like the "fair-locked goddess," daughter of Helios (the Sun) and of the Oceanide, Perse. James V., the father of Mary, was a Sun, in intellect and intention, among his unlettered nobility and subjects, and from him his daughter derived all those brilliant characteristics for which she is extolled. From her mother, Mary of Guise, she inherited certain solid qualities which momentarily seemed to invest her with a power truly masculine—nay, at times almost superhuman—in meeting difficulty and confronting danger and death. These properties doubtless inclined her to the "REAL MAN," James Hepburn, the fearless, the faithful, and the phœnix amid the general reverse about her. What Ulysses was to Circe, Bothwell was to Mary, and just as the mythical enchantress became much attached to the unfortunate Greek hero and held him in the bondage of her superhuman blandishments for about a year, even so the intimate connection between Mary and Bothwell began to exhibit its passionate fervor shortly after the murder of Rizzio,—which occurred on the night of the 9th-10th March, 1566,—and terminated by their forcible separation at Carberry Hill, on the 15th June, 1567. Tennyson's strong but exquisite verses—a soliloquy which he attributes to the King of Ithaca—might serve as an equally apposite utterance for the Scottish Earl. Nay more, the Odyssey does not relate stranger *natural* adventures—casting aside the fabulous— than befell James Hepburn ; with the final fatal difference that Ulysses at the close found a fond and constant wife, hoping against hope, to welcome his restoration to her arms, whereas Bothwell perished in a distant prison, abandoned by an inconstant, intriguing consort, forgetful of her faithful knight and devoted worshiper in a new-born inane and insane passion for a far lesser man, the silly Duke of Norfolk.

Ulysses on the rocky shore of Ithaca—Bothwell on the storm-beat ramparts of Dunbar—about to sail forth to his fearful doom—speaks :

> " It little profits that an idle [Erle],
> By this still hearth, among these barren crags,
> Match'd with a wife [no mate],[6] I mete and dole
> Unequal laws unto a savage race,
> That hoard, and sleep, and feed, and know not me.
> I cannot rest from travel : *I will drink*
> *Life to the lees :* all times I have enjoy'd
> Greatly, have suffer'd greatly, both with those

[6] Whoever, without bias, studies the occurrences of this epoch, must recognize that the marriage of Bothwell with Jane Gordon was one rather of policy than of affection, because the Earl's passion for Mary manifested itself clearly long before this union was brought about by the Queen. The question of why, if Mary had any predilection for Bothwell and already hated Darnley, she favored a result which was apparently so inimical to a future connection with the man who was gradually winning his way deeper and deeper into her heart of hearts, has been answered by Burton with his usual skill in solving a number of historical riddles. " It was a political alliance for strengthening the cause of the Queen and her husband" (iv. 126). "The interest taken by Queen Mary in this marriage has been pitted against the many presumptions that *her heart then belonged to Bothwell.* But *experience in poor human nature teaches us that people terrified by the pressure of temptation do sometimes set up barriers against it which they afterwards make frantic efforts to get over*" (iv. 139). Jane Gordon had her vicissitudes, but the way in which she took them showed a quiet *spirit, fitted to make the best of existing conditions*" (iv. 219-2). Bothwell's wife was no sooner satisfied that a competence would be secured to her than she was perfectly willing to yield up and release her husband to gratify his wishes and those of the Queen. Chalmers (i. 160) says she " brought a suit with equal alacrity," the more willingly that the divorce was to insure and augment the pecuniary and political condition of her brother, the Earl of Huntley, and her other kin. The marriage and the divorce were both matters of bargain and sale. " *An dabit ?*" " *Dabitur !*"

That loved me, and alone ; on shore, and when
Thro' scudding drifts the rainy Hyades
Vext the dim sea : I am become a name ;
For always roaming with a *hungry* heart.
Much have I seen and known ; cities of men
And manners, climates, councils, governments,
Myself not least, but honor'd of them all ;
And drunk delight of battle with my peers,
*   *   *   *   *   *   *
Yet all experience is an arch where thro'
Gleams that untravel'd world, whose margin fades
Forever and forever when I move.
How dull it is to pause, to make an end,
To rust unburnish'd, not to shine in use !
As tho' to breathe were life.   Life piled on life
Were all too little, . . .
Little remains : but every hour is saved
From that eternal silence, something more,
A bringer of new things ; and vile it were
For some three suns to store and hoard myself,
And this gray spirit yearning in desire
To follow knowledge, like a sinking star,
Beyond the utmost bound of human thought.
*   *   *   *   *   *   *
There gloom the dark broad seas. My mariners,
Souls that have toil'd, and wrought, and thought with me—
That ever with a frolic welcome took
The thunder and the sunshine, and opposed
Free hearts, free foreheads—· . . .
Death closes all ; but something ere the end,
Some work of noble note, may yet be done,
Not unbecoming men that strove with Gods.
          . . . Come, my friends,
'Tis not too late to seek a newer world.
Push off, and sitting well in order smite
The sounding furrows ; for my purpose holds
To sail beyond the sun [rise] . . .
                    Until I die.
It may be that the gulfs will wash us down :
It may be we shall touch the Happy Isles.
Tho' much is taken, much abides ; and tho'
We are not now that strength which in old days
Moved earth and heaven, *that which we are, we are:*
One equal temper of heroic hearts,
Made weak by time and FATE, *but strong in will*
To strive, to seek, to find, and not to yield."

Mary, torn by rebel force and serpent guile from the side of the husband of her choice at Carberry Hill, 15th June, 1567, expiated her foolish confidence in the pledges of a subject who was either the obtuse tool of a vile aristocratic faction or a willing factor in one of the most cruel and atrocious plots ever engendered in the black hearts of a bold and cunning, but sordid and soulless, confederacy of " irreconcilable" magnates. General history with its usual *unreal* counterfeit (Victor

Hugo's "*menechme*") of truth, but its ordinary *real* perversion of facts, accepts Kirkaldy of Grange as the type of a chivalric soldier, knight, and gentleman. Those who have investigated closely deny to him the principles consistent with such a character, and charge that he was no better than a subsidized spy and agent of the Ministers of Elizabeth, the deadly enemies of his country and his sovereign, and a man who, under the mask of truth and honor, was no better than a courageous and able military setter-in-array-of-battle. Whether himself betrayed and betrayer, or "betrayer and betrayed," Mary owed to his impulse the fatal fall which toppled her over into the abyss. In her first plunge she caught on the sharp walls of Lochleven Castle, enjoyed a short spasm of hope when she escaped through the devotion of the bold George and the "little Willie" Douglas, was again thrust down into the darker depth through the principal instrumentality of the same Kirkaldy of Grange at Langside, 15th May, 1568, whence she fell deeper and deeper into the weary heart-wrench—that captivity of eighteen years—which ended on the block at the age of forty-four, in Fotheringay Castle, 8th February, 1587.

Seeing that this article is intended rather as a vindication of the calumniated Bothwell[7] than a narrative, *seriatim*, of the career of Mary, she must become a secondary personage in the consideration in order to compress what is necessary to rehabilitate the Earl within the space accorded. Therefore, with reference to the single incident in her life almost unknown to the reading public and scarcely revealed until within the year, the reader must pass to more prosaic matter. It has been claimed and urged with intense feeling, and argued with a bitterness which demonstrates that a verdict, just or unjust, was the only object, that Mary regretted her marriage with Bothwell. The exact contrary is the truth. Mary had a perfect opportunity to escape from him when the rebels, her pretended friends and his enemies, invested Borthwick Castle. Bothwell got away before the stronghold was completely invested, Mary rejected the invitation of those who claimed to be her rescuers from outrage, and disguised and mounted as a man, she fled by night to throw herself into the arms of her expectant husband. "She only entreated that she might be put on board of a ship with her husband, and left to drift wherever fortune might lead her." She represented "how much they wronged her in desiring to separate her from her husband, with whom she thought to live and die in the

[7] In preparing these remarks upon this extraordinary man Bothwell, a large number of authorities have been examined and a careful analysis of their views presented,—results of the most careful criticism. The immediate conclusion is in some measure a free translation—with interesting episodes from other sources—of the brief and argument of Dr. Phil A. Petrick (Berlin—St. Petersburg, 1874). whose labors have been almost exhaustive. His final decision on the most important points in controversy reverses almost every other judgment hitherto published, and, as a whole, is most favorable to Bothwell.

greatest happiness," " nor will consent by any persuasion to abandon Bothwell for her husband, but answereth constantly that she will live and die with him; and said that if it were put to her choice to re- linquish her crown and kingdom or Bothwell, she would leave her kingdom and dignity to live as a simple demoiselle with him, and that she will never consent that he shall be worse off or have more harm than herself." " They parted, as we are told, like fond lovers with many kisses, and much sorrow on her part."—(Burton, iv. 246.) She was scarcely separated from him when she wrote to him a letter which greatly aggravated her sorry situation; she strove, again and again, to send letters to him from Lochleven Castle; and her first thought was of him after her escape from its grim dungeon, and the first act of her freedom was to send off a messenger to seek him out. wherever he might be and *let him know that she was free* and craved a reunion with the lord of her heart and person.

Such passages might be multiplied, but to the point. When Eliza- beth, touched at length with pity at the forlorn condition of her sister queen, sent her agent, Throckmorton, to Scotland, he reported that she would not renounce Bothwell as a husband, that " she will by no means yield to abandon Bothwell for her husband, nor relinquish him, which matter will do her most harm of all, and hardens those Lords to great severity against her."

Furthermore, she clung to him because she was with child by him. Here is a mystery and as great a one, although not so well known, as that of the famous " Iron Mask" of the time of Louis XIV. Both are even yet unsolved and now perhaps insoluble. What is known of this child?

Lingard (v. 90 (2)), citing three authorities; Rapen (1733), ii. 83 (2); Miss Agnes Strickland, in her "Life of Mary Stuart," edition ii. vol. ii. p. 58; and Burton (Scribner and Welford's Edition), iv. 362–3, and notes 1 and 2, and others either refer to or furnish particu- lars as to this child—

> " Poor scapegoat of crimes, where—her part what it may,
>   So tortured, so hunted to die;
> Foul age of deceit and of hate—on her head
>   Least stains of gore-guiltiness lie;
> To the hearts of the just her blood from the dust
>   Not in vain for mercy will cry.
>
> " Poor scapegoat of nations and faiths in their strife,
>   So cruel—and thou so fair!
> Poor girl! so best, in her misery named—
>   Discrowned of two kingdoms, and bare;
> Not first nor last on this one was cast
>   The burden that others should share"—

whose career is worked up into the novel " UNKNOWN TO HISTORY," by Charlotte M. Yonge, author of the "Heir of Redclyffe," etc., of which the *Preface* bears date 27th February, 1882. At page 99, and note annexed, in the writer's "Study," "Mary, Queen of Scots," given to the public about the 1st February, 1882, nearly a month previous to the date of Miss Yonge's Preface, the particulars of the Birth and Fate of this child are presented. Raumer, in his "Queen Elizabeth and Queen Mary," Letter XXI., quotes the correspondence of the English Envoy on this subject.

Labanoff, or his Editor, under date 1568, states: "In February (nine months after marriage), Marie Stuart gives birth at Lochleven to a daughter, who is taken to France, where she becomes afterwards a Nun at Notre de Soissons."

The note to this reads as follows: "The pregnancy of the Queen of Scotland has been denied by Gilbert Stuart, who wrote in 1782; but Dr. Lingard, having reproduced this fact as unshaken in his history of England, I have considered myself compelled to adopt his version, relying especially on the testimony of Le Laboureur, a very praiseworthy historian, who, in his additions to the Memoires of Castelnau (French Ambassador to Scotland at the time), vol. i. p. 610, edition of 1731, speaks of the daughter of Marie Stuart. [This is the Castelnau to whom Agnes Strickland, in her "Life of Mary Stuart," alludes in such very high terms.]

"It must be remembered that the author (Le Laboureur) cited, filled a post of confidence at the Court of France (he was Counsellor and Almoner to the King), and that he had every means of knowing the different particulars kept secret for so long a time. Besides, when he published his work it was easy for him to consult the Registers of the Convent of Notre Dame de Soissons, and to assure himself in fact if the daughter of Marie Stuart had been a Nun therein."

There is no portrait of Bothwell, but wherever he is represented in pictures, he always appears like what Petrick styles him, "A REAL MAN." It will be shown in the course of this article that he not only had great mental power, but that for his time his education had been anything but neglected. The panegyrist of the falsest of false Scottish nobles, the Regent Murray,—whom Mary so hated that she granted a pension to his murderer,—is scarcely more complimentary to Bothwell than one of the most zealous advocates of Mary, while others who have examined into the facts dispassionately depict the Earl as a fallen angel, but still invested with all the glorious outer attractions of one of the highest of the condemned celestial hierarchy. According to Dargand and his school, Bothwell was worthy the imagery of "Paradise Lost":

> "—— and next him Moloch, scepter'd king,
> Stood up, the strongest and the fiercest spirit
> That fought in Heav'n, now fiercer by despair:
> His trust was with th' Eternal to be deem'd

Equal in strength, and rather than be less
Car'd not to be at all; with that care lost
Went all his fear; of God, or Hell, or worse
He reck'd not, and these words thereafter spake.
My sentence is for open war: of wiles,
More unexpert, I boast not: them let those
Contrive who need, or when they need, not now.

*   *   *   *   *   *   *   *

On this side nothing; and by proof we feel
Our pow'r sufficient to disturb his Heav'n,
And with perpetual inroads to alarm,
Though inaccessible, his fatal throne:
Which if not victory is yet revenge.
He ended frowning, and his look denounc'd
Desperate revenge, and battel dangerous
To less than gods. On th' other side uprose
Belial,—[Murray]—in act more graceful and humane;
A fairer person lost not Heav'n; he seem'd
For dignity compos'd and high exploit:
But all was false and hollow; though his tongue
Dropt manna, and could make the worse appear
The better reason,—"

Here is a very apposite contrast between Bothwell (Moloch), audacious, fearless, fiery, and impulsive, and Murray (Belial), sleek, cunning, cautious, brave, *but not bold*, and plausible.

*   *   *   *   *   *   *   *   *

In the forenoon of the 6th October, 1566, Bothwell started for the Borders, where a serious disturbance demanded his presence, in advance of the Queen. The Armstrongs, Elliots, and Johnstons ("Border-ruffians" we would style them to-day) were at war with each other. It was on this occasion that he was himself severely wounded in a personal encounter with John Elliot, of Park, a noted Borderer, whom some call a robber, others an insurgent. According to Chalmers (ii. 108), Elliot had some claim to the succession of the Hermitage. This could scarcely be, since it was an hereditary appanage of the Hepburns. Bothwell, however, despite his own wounds, finally killed Elliot after a protracted and exceptional struggle. Partly from error, partly from ill-will, this affair has been very much misrepresented. Bothwell's personal courage has even been assailed by his inveterate calumniators, particularly the vile Buchanan, or the adventure set aside as being romance. The very antagonism of his calumniators establishes Bothwell's worth, for "*it must not be forgotten that the Border warriors were not to be influenced except by personal bravery.*" A few days later, but as soon as circumstances permitted, " Mary flew, as it were, with the impatience of a lover," to visit Bothwell.

Did Mary hasten to the side of her severely wounded Lieutenant-General in obedience to the yearning of affection, or simply in response to the promptings of gratitude for peril encountered in her service and admiration of a duty gallantly performed? To any student who has had experience of life,—not the humdrum career of the respectable—so styled—citizen, but of the man of the world,—to any one who has been not only "a looker-on in Vienna," but a participant in the varied enjoyments which that capital affords, Mary's motive could have been neither more nor less than the passion which furnishes the theme of one of the most agreeable of recent operettas, in which the most charming chorus rings with

> "'Tis love! love! love!"

More argument has been devoted to this question than it would appear, at first blush, to deserve, but the consequences were eventually momentous. To ordinary readers it seems a mere episode, because few are aware that the fate of English Protestantism hinged on the connection of Mary with Bothwell. That it did so is ably shown by a careful statement of cause and effect, as set forth clearly in a remarkable book entitled "The Coming Man," published in London in 1881. As a consideration preliminary to the visit to the Hermitage it is necessary to investigate when Mary began to evince that partiality for Bothwell which developed unto a honeymoon but a few hours longer than a lunar month and terminated in life-long misery to both. According to the judgment of those who seek to defend or clear up the character of the Queen, her affection for Bothwell cannot be traced back much more than a year, and flamed out after the murder of Rizzio, 9th March, 1566. One argument in favor of this view, apparently unanswerable, is her permitting him to marry Lady Jane Gordon, 24th February, 1566. Burton (iv. 139) deprives this plea of any force. Comparing dates and indications, the Queen's partiality for the Earl can be followed back— as a savage detects and pursues a trail—to the period when, after her return from France in 1561, she had grasped the sceptre firmly. The miserable Darnley episode flared up like the firing of a dry brush-heap and sunk into embers even before the murder of her favorite secretary, to be extinguished with the indignant tears wrung from her fair eyes by that worse than useless crime. From this time forward, Bothwell was the first man in Scotland, and when in consequence of the performance of his duty as Warden of the Marches he lay dying, as was supposed,—in his ancestral stronghold and official headquarters, the "Hermitage,"— Mary galloped thither from Jedburgh, "a stiff twenty miles' journey." This estimate of the distance is small, because she did not take the shortest route. If the tradition be true, she made a circuit and was nearly lost in a dangerous morass, still called the "Queen's Mire." Into this her famous white palfrey plunged and was with difficulty extricated. The ride is really much longer; nearly, if not fully, twenty-four miles. As she returned to Jedburgh on the same day, it was a feat that must have tested the endurance of a practiced rider. Sir Walter Scott, who is by no means favorable on any occasion to Bothwell, admits that it is an open question " whether she (the Queen) visited a wounded subject, or a lover in danger." The Wizard of the North adds : " The *Queen's Mire* is still a pass of danger, exhibiting, in many places, the bones of the horses which have been entangled in it. For what reason the Queen chose to enter Liddesdale, by the circuitous route of Hawick, is not told. There are other two passes from Jedburgh to Hermitage Castle ; the one by the *Note of the Gate*, the other over the mountain called Winburgh. Either of these, but especially the latter, is several miles shorter than that by Hawick and the *Queen's Mire*. But, by the circuitous way of Hawick, the Queen could traverse the districts of more friendly clans than by going directly into the disorderly province of Liddesdale."

Mary's self-constituted champions furthermore insist, to divest the expedition of any remarkable character, that this ride occurred at a fine season of the year. If there were positive records that the weather was absolutely or unseasonably fine on that particular day, it might be an argument and a proof. Without such evidence to the contrary, it is well known that the weather in the region traversed, late in October, is as a rule anything but propitious for female equestrianism. Even after a lapse of over three centuries Burton (iv. 177), who has walked over the ground, states : " The author [Burton] knows, from having walked over the ground, that Hermitage Castle is a stiff twenty miles' journey [direct road for a pedestrian] from Jedburgh."

The Queen remained two hours, " to Bothwell's great pleasure and content," with him. After she had galloped back, twenty to twenty-four miles or even more, to Jedburgh, despite her fatigue, she spent a great part of the night writing to Bothwell; some say on business, others from affection. Lingard attempts to demonstrate that a woman —especially one who had undergone great fatigue all the previous day —who had just spent hours with her lover would not be likely to waste the hours which should be devoted to rest in writing to him, the more particularly when she could see this lover the next day if she chose, or might reasonably expect to see him very soon. This argument appeared to be inconsequential and weak even to the phlegmatic German, Raumer, who remarks thereupon that if it proves anything it proves clearly that Lingard, himself, had never been in love. Whatever motive actuated the Queen in what she did, the result of the anxiety, fatigue, and the preceding and subsequent labors was a fever which very nearly proved fatal to her.

From this time forward any one who doubts that Mary's passion for the Earl was growing more and more irresistible, knows nothing of life and nothing of women. The great barrier between them was Darnley. Nothing could demolish that but death. That he was to die was soon determined. Simply the "how" and the "when" remained to be decided. When the plan was arranged, Mary lured him to his place of doom. Little search is needed to find proofs that Bothwell's wife constituted an obstacle of little consequence. The lands of her brother, the Earl of Huntley, had been confiscated. He was seeking their restoration. Lady Jane seems to have been perfectly willing to make a fair bargain to get herself out of the way. There was collusion all around. The great feudal nobility,—a precious set of rascals, than whom a more mean, cruel, self-seeking, totally unprincipled set scarcely appear, elsewhere, in history,—for divers reasons, wanted to be rid of Darnley as King-Consort; Mary desired to be quit of him as a husband; Bothwell as a rival, *in chances* if not in the heart of the woman he loved, and all the rest, closely or remotely concerned, were perfectly willing to do all that was required to be done to show themselves agreeable to all parties.

In spite of the hundreds of volumes that have been published on this subject, and the still more numerous articles, Darnley did not lose his life by the measures taken by Bothwell, or by the hands or violence of the Earl's own personal following. Goodhall proclaimed the fact a good many years ago and was laughed at for it: " but Mr. Goodhall has adopted the most ridiculous and extravagant hypothesis of all, and has endeavored to prove that even Bothwell was not the murderer." Theodor Opitz, *Freiburg im Breisgau*, 1879, in his "Maria Stuart," 170–2, and Dr. Ernst Bekker (*Giessen*), 1881, in his "Maria Stuart, Darly, [which Dr. Petrick maintains as the proper spelling of the name], Bothwell," 67–83, demonstrate conclusively that, notwithstanding all the sneering at his conclusion, Goodhall was right. Unquestionably Bothwell was guilty in intent. But, what says Shakspeare on "Intent" ("Measure for Measure," V. 1):

> " His act did not o'ertake his bad intent ;
> And must be buried but as an intent
> That perished by the way : thoughts are no subjects.
> Intents but merely thoughts."

These are the real facts:

There (at Kirk of Field) Darnley had gone to bed an hour after the departure of the Queen. Alongside of him slept his old servant, William Taylor ; two others, Thomas Nelson and Edward Simons, lay in the hall ; two grooms on the ground-floor next the bedroom sometimes occupied by the Queen. Between two and three o'clock in the morning an explosion took place. With a frightful report the house of the Prebendary Balfour flew into the air.

The occurrences immediately before that hour are veiled by a darkness which will perhaps never be quite dispelled. If one reads the declarations of Hepburn and Hay, Bothwell remained with them to the last. At two o'clock, they say, they lighted the match, shut the doors behind them, and retired to where Bothwell stood some little distance off. They describe him as devoured with impatience ; they had to show him a window through which he could see the glimmering of the match ;

indeed, he wished, they say, as the explosion continued to delay, to go into the house; but Hepburn held him back. At last the so impatiently expected thunder shook the air and ground. Not until now, by their account, did Bothwell with his assistants and servants start upon their return to Edinburgh, in spite of many hindrances soon reached his home, and, after taking something to drink, laid himself down in bed with his wife. But it is scarcely possible that he accomplished the distance (several (three) miles) on foot in so short a time as to have been in bed already half an hour, when those inhabiting Holyrood, startled from sleep by the tremendous report, got up; and a court officer, who from terror could not speak a word, awoke him. *Probably he, at the latest, left* the Kirk of Field *when the match was kindled.*

However this may be, the death of Darnley was not caused by the explosion, arranged by Bothwell; and, also, the house could not have been so thoroughly destroyed as it was by the powder scattered about by Hepburn, Hay, and Ormistoun. Its complete ruin, extending to the very foundation walls, is to be explained by the *mines dug and loaded*—perhaps *without Bothwell's* knowledge—by Maitland, Balfour, and Archibald Douglas, which too took fire and exploded.

But what was the end of Darnley? His corpse, near that of his valet William Taylor, was found about five o'clock in the morning, under a tree, in an orchard, and about eighty yards (two hundred and forty feet) away from the house. Both bodies were entirely uninjured, no trace of wounds from burning or contusion. The King was clothed only with his shirt,—near him lay a fur coat and his slippers. Melvil mentions, in his memoirs, the story of a page, to the effect that Darnley was attacked when asleep, dragged out, and near a stable was strangled with a napkin. The Count Moretta, on the other hand, was of opinion that the King, woke up by the murderers moving about the house, and by the creaking of the doors opened with false keys, in his shirt, and with the fur coat in his hand, tried to escape with Taylor through a door leading into the garden, but was held fast, strangled, and carried into the neighboring orchard. But one does not see why the murderers should have taken the trouble to bring both bodies so far from the house and over a wall, instead of abandoning them, with the other people in the house, to destruction by the explosion. It seems, therefore, more natural to assume that Darnley and Taylor actually succeeded in escaping through the garden and in getting over the wall, but were pursued and strangled under the fruit-trees where they were found. In the excitement and confusion they were left lying there.

The murderers of the King were neither Bothwell nor his three artificers; but the greatest probability speaks for the contrary,—*i.e.*, [implicates] Morton's representative, the Castellan of Whittingham, Archibald Douglas, with his servants John Binning and Thomas Gairner, the three men in slippers whom Powrie and Wilson met at Black-Friars. A slipper was found among the ruins and recognized as the one which, according to the declaration of Binning and Gairner, Archibald Douglas had lost. Beside this, some women, living in the vicinity of the orchard, bore witness before the Privy Council that they heard a cry, "Ah, my brother, pity me for the love of Him who pities us all!" On the mother's side Darnley was a relation of Douglas. Other conspirators, too, were on the scene. Thus Binning thought that he recognized the voice of the Prebendary Robert Balfour among the masked persons whom he met on the street subsequent to the explosion; whereupon John Maitland, Abbot of Coldingham, and brother of the Secretary of State, recommending silence, closed his mouth. The women mentioned saw groups of eight and eleven persons go towards the city in the greatest haste. Drury, however, gives Cecil, on the 24th April, 1567, from Berwick, the following details, which he probably heard from Murray, who just before that date went to the continent by way of Berwick: "It was Captain Cullen who gave the advice to make things more sure by strangling the King and not to rely on the powder only, a thing which, he asserted, he had seen many a one escape. Sir Andrew Kerr (of Faudonside), had ridden to the place in order to help in the bloody deed, if necessary. It was a long time before the King died. He defended his life with all his strength."

The valet Nelson affords, in fact, the proof of the correctness of Cullen's remark,—he was pulled out of the ruins alive.

Thus much is translated from Opitz, 1879. Bekker[s] goes much more into details, with further proofs, and demonstrates and confirms

[s] DEATH OF DARNLEY. By Dr. Ernest Bekker.—(The point) that neither Bothwell nor his people took any personal share in the strangling of the King because the spot on which they were posted prevented their doing so, finds its confirmation in the extremely noteworthy fact that all of Bothwell's followers who were executed as murderers of the King declared before death repeatedly and in the most solemn manner that they had gone away from the Kirk of Field in the firm conviction that the King had perished in the explosion. The Laird of Ormistoun, who was not present at the explosion, relates in his deposition that he also had no other idea than that the King was buried under the ruins of the house, and that he had in the most careful manner questioned Hay and Hepburn, as well as all the others of Bothwell's people who were that night at the Kirk of Field, concerning the killing of the King, and that they all swore to him that they had never supposed anything else than that the King was killed by the explosion. These men said the same thing in full view of death, and, singularly enough, this declaration has not been altered, though it was so damaging; for it follows from it, first, that Bothwell and his people were at a spot where they could hear nothing of what was happening in the garden situated to the south of the court; second, that this spot cannot possibly have been other than the Thief Raw (the wynd beside the Black-Friars,—deposition of Dalgleish of the 3d January, 1568), for at every other spot behind the city wall any one could, and must, hear what took place at eighty paces distance from the house.

Bothwell's people knew nothing because, in accordance with the orders of their master, they watched or guarded the Thief Raw, at a considerable distance from the garden, and in addition were separated from the place of the murder by the high city wall. Hay and Hepburn for their part could at first know nothing more about the murder, because that during this time they were with Bothwell in the cellar attending to the powder.

Not the Earl of Bothwell, but others must have strangled the King. Circumstances prove that he had the special charge of conducting the explosion and of watching the house on that side from which alone the powder could be taken into the cellar, so that he with his six companions was divided from the scene of the murder by the town wall. But independent of this, it was utterly impossible that Bothwell could carry out such an undertaking alone. Would the Scottish nobility, who in the sixteenth century possessed a great mastery of organizing and carrying out conspiracies, have committed the execution of such an uncommonly risky enterprise to a single noble with six followers? In case things did not go well it might come to a desperate struggle, in which the King with his six servants might defend himself successfully. Could the chiefs of the Scottish nobility, and especially the chiefs of the conspiracy, the cunning Maitland, Argyle, Huntley, Morton, Murray, and James Balfour, be so foolish as not to take the most extreme measures of precaution in an undertaking whose failure would ruin them in life and property? Could they, the actual originators and plotters of the murder, sleep quietly on that night in which either the life of the King was to be offered up or in which their own lives, in case of a miscarriage or discovery, would fall into the deadliest danger? These questions must be answered with a decided negative, and the result shows that all provisionary measures which could render miscarriage impossible were attended to.

Matter-of-fact proofs and clues showing that yet other highly-placed personages participated in the murder are to be found in abundance in the material on hand, but they have been as little collected as those which show that the Earl of Bothwell

his German *confrère* of the pen.   He wrote as late as 1881, with still
more published evidence for his guidance.

This clearly exonerates Bothwell of everything but the intent; in

with a couple of assistants neither did nor could have carried out this daring act
alone.

William Powrie says in his deposition that at one time, with Wilson, at the
unlading of the powder, he met Paris with two masked persons ; a certain proof
that there were yet other suspicious persons who went about the Kirk of Field on
that night.   On his second hearing Powrie said that, as they brought the last load
of powder, Bothwell came to him in company with three others who wore cloaks
and silk overshoes.   It is out of the question, however, that Bothwell should have
been present at the unlading of the powder, since he was, precisely at this time,
with the other Lords paying a visit to the King.   This declaration of Powrie has in
any case been tampered with.   Powrie can only have seen those three persons with
Bothwell when the latter went a second time to the Kirk of Field for the purpose
of giving the order for lighting the match.   And that these three wore silk overshoes shows that they were noble, perhaps Lords, for silk overshoes were at that
time, in Scotland, only worn by the nobility, and especially by those among them
who lived at Court.

In exact correspondence with these declarations is the confession of John Binning, a servant of Archibald Douglas, in the year 1581, before his execution as
a regicide.   In the memorable fragment of Binning's confession it is said that A.
Douglas with his servants, Binning and Gairner, went to the Kirk of Field for
the purpose of performing the deed.   Archibald had on silk overshoes, and when he
came in changed his clothes, which were covered with mud and dirt.   Binning, who
was sent to Throplow's Wynd, undoubtedly to look after the other murderers, who
were hastening home, met certain masked men, among whom he thought he recognized the voice of Robert Balfour.   There came also John Maitland, Abbot of
Coldingham, and brother of the Secretary, who gave Binning a sign to keep silence
by laying his hand upon his (own) mouth.

Douglas was covered with mud and dirt when he came home.   Thus he could
not have been if he were a mere looker-on, but only if he, possibly, had stumbled
in the flight or had taken part in a fight.   The former is possible, the last certain.
A fight of desperation took place between the murderers on one side, and the King,
with his page, Taylor, on the other side.   But more of this, as also of the masked
men, farther on.

Another account as regards the murderers who fled towards the city comes
from two women who woke up, in a fright, at the fearful report and rushed out of
doors.   Both deposed at their examination that they had counted nineteen persons who were running in the direction of the town.   One of these women, Mag.
Crockat, tried in vain to stop one of the fugitives, who had on a silken garment,
and was therefore one of the courtiers.

The Earl of Murray, who not long after the murder of the King set off for
France, had (on his way thither, during his stay in London) an interview with the
Spanish Ambassador, de Silva, during which he informed the ambassador that there
were thirty to forty persons, in one way or another, mixed up in the murder.   Murray here does not reckon himself among the guilty, as Morton also, at a later period,
according to the peculiar ideas of the Scottish nobility, did not reckon himself.   By
the guilty he meant, not those privy to the conspiracy, but those who took an active
part in it; and among these, again, especially those who were present at the act of
murder.   Further, Murray probably did not intend in his thirty to forty persons
to include servants and subordinate actors of lower rank, but the nobles among the
conspirators, for he speaks of the "guilty parties."   Among the conspirators were
the murderers of Riccio.   The condition on which Murray, Maitland, Athol, Argyle,

this he was no more guilty than Murray, Morton, and a number of others the highest in rank, position, and influence. Murray, the hypocrite, was just as guilty in respect to intent as Bothwell, and before an

Huntley, and Bothwell promised to use their influence for their pardon on account of Riccio's murder was their joining the conspiracy against the King's life; and as we have seen, Morton, his friends, and followers at Newcastle, joyfully acceded to the "bond" of Craigmillar. The murderers of Riccio bore a deadly hatred to Darnley as a traitor, and one of them, who, in December, 1566, had not been pardoned, Ker of Faudonside, put freedom and life at stake in order to feast his eyes upon the murder of the King. He rode in the night—9th–10th February—with several companions to that suburb of Edinburgh, and after having seen the explosion, returned back again to the Border. If a banished Riccio-murderer risked this, one may conclude that the returned ones were ready to do it, particularly as they were actual conspirators. This one circumstance points at something which, considering the preceding circumstances, is more than probable.

Kirk of Field lay in the suburb. Since, now, without the slightest doubt, the house was surrounded on all sides, the supposition is very ready that the murderers of the King did not, all of them, approach it from the city, but that also a part came thither from the country; for one could reach the house quite as easily, perhaps more easily, from this last direction as from the city, and one was much less likely to be noticed. A body of horsemen on their way to the chief city attracted no attention, it was a common object.

The instance of Ker of Faudonside proves on the one hand that the death-hour of the King was exactly known to the individual members of the wide-branching conspiracy, and allows one to conclude with certainty, on the other hand, that if, beside this Faudonside, other nobles had come from the country to the Kirk of Field, they did this, not merely as idle spectators to quench their thirst for revenge with the murder-scene, but also with the definite purpose of investing the Kirk of Field on this side (South and East), and in case of need themselves pushing in. It is possible that Murray's sudden leaving of Edinburgh on the 9th February was connected with this circumstance, and did not come simply from the intention of diverting from himself a suspicion of participation in the murder.

It cannot be doubted from the adduced facts that the murder of Darnley, exactly as the murder of Riccio, was carried out by a great number of persons, and that the subsequent, commonly accepted, story that Bothwell, with a few subordinate assistants of the lower rank, accomplished a wildly desperate adventure is simply laughable. . . . The fact is entirely lost or forgotten or out of sight that a conspiracy of the highest magnates of the state, and of nearly all the Calvinistic nobles, had been formed in December, 1566, and January, 1567, with the closest secrecy and entirely independent. . . .

Binning's confession shows that Archibald Douglas, John Maitland, the brother of the Secretary, and Robert Balfour, the brother of James Balfour, took part in the murder. But these were not the only ones. It is almost certain that the above-named pair of brothers were with Argyle at the Kirk of Field on that night, and Huntley's participation is quite certain.

When Bothwell took his trusted servant Paris into the secret, he said, among many other things, "I have Lethington, who is considered one of the best heads in this country, and who is the manager of the whole. Besides, there are in the affair my brother-in-law Argyle, Huntley, Morton, Ruthven, and Lindsay." The three last named were not then in Edinburgh, but probably the three first were, and, as we have seen, were at the noticeable visit to the Kirk of Field on the evening of the 9th of February.

That Maitland should be called the "manager of the whole" agrees exactly with his conduct at Craigmillar, where he showed himself with Murray as properly

5

English or a New Jersey judge and jury would have been held as amenable. In New York, where the application of the law has degenerated so low as to make angels weep, Murray might have escaped

the originator and maker of the conspiracy. It also agrees with the circumstance that Maitland recommended the house of Robert Balfour, in the Kirk of Field, to the Queen, and indicates that the whole plan of the murder sprang from his brain.

Again we have another piece of testimony, from which his guilt, indirectly, appears. When Morton, at the end of 1572, became Regent, Maitland, who then was a warm partisan of the Queen, protested, in a memorial to the new Regent, against being declared an outlaw " for a crime whereof he (Morton) knoweth in his conscience I was as innocent as himself." Morton answered in the following remarkable way : " That I know him innocent in my conscience as myself, the contrary thereof is true, for I was and am innocent thereof, but could not affirm the same of him, considering what I understand in that matter of his own confession to myself of before."

Laing thinks that Morton alludes to the negotiations which took place between Maitland, Bothwell, and Morton, at Whittingham, on the 20th of January, 1567. This cannot be. At that time either one of the three named was as guilty as the others, since the murder was not yet perpetrated. It is said that Morton was persuaded at Whittingham to take part in the murder, which he had previously refused to do because the promised written assent of the Queen could not be procured. The Earl of Morton had the same idea of " guilty" that Murray had in talking with de Silva. He did not reckon those who concealed a crime, but the actual perpetrators only, as really guilty ; he means by the words " by his own confession to myself of before" not a conference before the murder, but a confession concerning the commission of it. It was the words " of before" which led Laing into error. Without any reason he thinks this " earlier" must mean before the 9th of February, 1567, and forgets that Morton spoke these words towards the end of 1572. This nice distinction which Morton makes between his participation and that of Maitland allows of but one interpretation,—*i e.*, that Morton had it from Maitland's own mouth that he was present at the carrying out of the crime, and was not, like Morton, simply privy to and a concealer and an abettor of the murder.

The participation of the Earl of Huntley in the murder is fully substantiated. " As Bothwell," says Paris, " was about to go the second time to the Kirk of Field, Huntley, with two or three servants, came to him in his chamber. After they had whispered a great deal the visitor left, and Bothwell said to Paris, who stood near, that Huntley had offered to accompany them, but he did not wish to take him." Huntley was nevertheless at the Kirk of Field that night. Therefore, either the wording of this declaration of Paris has been falsified, or Bothwell said this in order not to expose his friend before the servant.

Archibald Douglas, already mentioned as one of the murderers, told Morton, after the deed was completed, that he was present at the murder, and went with Huntley and Bothwell to the Kirk of Field.

Undoubtedly Huntley and Douglas were two of those three unnamed noblemen in mantles and silk overshoes whom Powrie at one time saw with Bothwell, and in any case upon the way to the Kirk of Field. Powrie certainly says, on his second hearing, that the same persons came to Bothwell during the unlading of the powder,—a lie, which is confuted by the deposition of Morton, and also, as already remarked, by the fact that these Lords, during the time the powder was put into the cellar, were making a visit to the King.

According to the deposition of Dalgleish, Bothwell, after the explosion, hastened as quickly as possible to his apartments, and, in order to awaken no suspicion, went to bed immediately. He had been there but a short time when a certain George Hacket entered the chamber for the purpose of telling him the shocking news of

because he was an available candidate and expert in political expediency. He was like an experienced burglar who "puts up the job," watches around the corner while the crime is being committed, and

the murder of the King. With this declaration Powrie's and Hepburn's depositions exactly agree, with the difference that the latter adds that Huntley also came immediately to Bothwell, and the former, that not alone Huntley, but also others appeared in the room, and that they all, from thence, betook themselves to the apartments of the Queen. These others, then, whose names Powrie, unhappily, has not mentioned, were noblemen, without doubt the leagued-lords, and among them Argyle and Maitland, who, as was usual with the bearers of high offices in Scotland, and just as did Bothwell and Huntley, lived in the royal palace.

This highly suspicious circumstance allows of only two explanations. If individual chiefs of the conspiracy remained that night behind in the palace, they knew what the detonation signified, but at the same time they could only guess about when the leaders of the undertaking would have got back to the palace; exactly when they could not know, since the murderers, in any case, were careful to get back to their apartments as secretly and as unnoticed as possible.

The meeting of the conspiring Lords in Bothwell's room, shortly after his return to the palace, is so striking that it may be explained by another yet more apparent conjecture. The Lords hit the time, when Bothwell had slipped home to his chamber, so precisely, because that, generally, they themselves could get there no sooner, having been at the Kirk of Field, as we know with certainty concerning Huntley.

Of the three in mantles and silk overshoes, whom Powrie saw with Bothwell upon the way to the Kirk of Field, two were Huntley and Archibald Douglas. Among the masked men ("certain mussilit men") whom Binning mentions was the brother of the advocate—J. Balfour,—John Maitland, the brother of the Secretary, came undisguised. The question is, who was that third nobleman of Powrie's, and who were the other masked men whom Binning saw? A noble murderer himself gives the answer (the already often mentioned Archibald Douglas), in his well-known, but yet little studied letter to Mary Stuart in Sheffield during the year 1581.

"The murder," writes Douglas, "was (done or executed) carried out by these persons, and took place at the command of those among the nobility who signed the league for this object;" that is to say, not alone Bothwell and Huntley, but also Argyle, Maitland, and James Balfour took part in the bloody work at the Kirk of Field. That third person was therefore Argyle.

What Douglas here writes is corroborated in fullest measure by other accounts. When the Laird Hay of Talla was imprisoned in September, 1567, he accused not only Huntley as a leader in the murder, but a great number of the most prominent Lords.

About Christmas, 1567, a number of Bothwell's people were taken prisoners in the Orkneys, as we are told, twelve or fifteen. Laing doubts this account, which we owe to Archbishop Beaton. He thinks that because in January, 1568, there were but four of Bothwell's people executed, there could not have been such a number of prisoners, especially since John Hepburn of Bolton was the only one among them guilty (of the murder).

The Earl of Morton, previous to his execution, named only Bothwell, Huntley, and Archibald Douglas as actually committing the murder. When he was asked concerning the other actors, he said, "I know none and will accuse none." Proof enough that he who through his whole life was one of the most tricky enemies of the Queen could very well have named others in addition.

It then stands established that Bothwell could not have singly carried out the murder, and also did not thus carry it out alone.

appropriates the best portion of the plunder. He counseled with the conspirators as to getting rid of Darnley, got out of the way when their plans were to be carried into execution, and he gave Bothwell a ban-

Thus viewed the confession of Binning unrolls quite another picture of the murder, with the names of other murderers. Binning names not a Hay, Hepburn Powrie, etc., but Archibald Douglas, John Maitland, Robert Balfour. Perhaps he, also, named other murderers of high standing, a circumstance which we owe to the probably fragmentary character of his confession. The servant of Douglas could name no other persons because he, with his master, Huntley, and the rest, stood on the other side of the city wall. Now it was on this side where Huntley, the Maitlands, the Balfours, Douglas, and in any case Argyle, also, stood that Darnley was strangled. Bothwell, on the contrary, had, from the other side of the city wall, gone into the cellar and examined the powder which Hay and Hepburn were guarding, while his four other servants stood at the point of commencement of the " Thief Raw." These circumstances, as already remarked, give the only clue to the fact that all Bothwell's people, both immediately after the murder (when questioned) by Ormistoun, and also at a later period, in the presence of death, declared, in the most solemn manner, that they hastened away from the Kirk of Field under the firm conviction that the King had been killed by the explosion.

Precisely in the fact, that this most important declaration of the unfortunate tools of Bothwell appears with the most perfect agreement in the depositions, lies the best guaranty for its truthfulness. The judges of these men had acted much more wisely if, instead of disfiguring their depositions by plump contradictions, or forcing them to false declarations by the rack, as is the case with the second deposition of Paris, they had thrown the strangling of the King directly upon Bothwell and his people. This the secret tribunal, which consisted of Morton, Maitland, Argyle, Huntley, and James Balfour, did not do; and this, perhaps, in order to make the mystery of this murder still more mysterious, by directing suspicion upon Bothwell only. But, perhaps, also from the fear that exasperation at too audacious lying might bring the other yet living murderers, or the friends of Bothwell, or perhaps Bothwell himself, some day to expose the true relation of things. Certain it is that the regicides entertained this fear when the Calvinistic noble party split. They accused each other mutually (that is, the two parties) of the murder of the King, but no one of the accusers (Argyle, Huntley, Murray, Maitland, James Balfour, etc.) dared to raise up the veil which lay over the commission of the deed; for had any one of those named done so he must have, always, feared that the accusation of a personal participation in the act of murdering the King would excite the accused to prove the same against the accuser. Each one preferred to pass as a member of the conspiracy in order not himself to be named as one of the actual perpetrators.

As regards the manner of the murder, this one explanation can alone appear trustworthy, according to the foregoing facts, namely, that Darnley or his page Taylor heard suspicious noises, or possibly, by chance, saw unaccustomed figures stealing about at the Kirk of Field. That in an attempt at flight through the neighboring gardens they ran into the hands of a group of murderers, who were lurking about under the leading of Huntley, of Balfour, or of the Maitlands, and of Archibald Douglas. Without doubt, the short struggle then took place, during which the King shouted those cries for help which were heard by some women in the neighborhood; and also, perhaps, the mud and dirt which covered the clothing of Archibald Douglas came from his participation in this struggle with the King and his page.

Of the other explanations, that one which Laing (chap. vii.) and Hume (chap. xxiv.) represent, viz., " the King and his page were thrown eighty ells by the ex-

quet, in his own house, when the miserable boy-king was a corpse. If *disinterested* and *impartial* men of ability ever rewrite the history of this time, Murray will not stand forth as a model worthy of imitation, any more than some political magnates in this country who have learned to pull the wires and command the " bar'ls" of their accomplices and dupes. Murray was a character which is not confined to his era. It is " for all time." Bothwell was a man of his own time, impossible at

plosion, without being singed," is simply laughable. A second, which Hosack (i. 268) mentions, along with the only true one, maintains, on the ground of a letter of W. Drury, is, that the King and his page Taylor were first strangled in the chamber, and then carried out of doors. This is quite as untenable, for, apart from the consideration that such a murder scene in the house would have woke up the servants, the murderers, in a business so pressing for haste, would hardly have taken the trouble to drag the bodies of the murdered eighty ells away from the house in the garden. The circumstance that the fur mantle and slippers of the King, as also some pieces of clothing belonging to Taylor, were lying not far from the corpses, proves that these articles were hurriedly taken up at the flight, and in the struggle were torn from them or lost; for to assume that the pieces of clothing which the murdered persons had on were not strewed about the garden until after the struggle would be contrary to sense.

Thus the King Henry was murdered, a sacrifice to the Calvinistic nobles-party to the revenge of the Riccio murderers, as well as to his own disrespectful behavior to the magnates of Scotland, with whom he should rather have sought sympathy and reconciliation than to show them, on every opportunity, his hatred and distrust. His murderers were the very persons who, on a ceremonious visit, laughing and flattering, surrounded him on the evening of the 9th February, 1567. They were those who, a few hours later, in the same night, entered the apartment of his wife with signs of the deepest condolence.

Let us now, in conclusion, review the results so far attained, which we must keep steadily in sight for what follows.

It results from certain reports which were written in the year 1566, and in the immediate surroundings of the Queen, that the position of isolation which Darnley assumed at that time, in respect to the Court, was a consequence, not of the hatred which his Consort is said to have thrown upon him, but a consequence of his enmity towards and his mistrust of the royal ministry. Darnley had a deadly anxiety lest his yielding wife should some day yield to the pressure of her ministers and amnesty the banished murderers of Riccio, whom he had so shamefully betrayed. It is most important for us that these things are confessed by the royal ministers themselves in a long account, dated 8th October, 1566, to Catharine de Medici, and it is quite as important that the Earls Huntley and Argyle, two of the King's murderers, at a later period declared, in a protest against Murray's usurped Regency, that the death of Darnley had been determined on by the chief of the nobility (the royal minister) at Craigmillar, because Darnley stood in the way of the pardon of the Riccio murderers. Out of the conspiracy of the ministers grew a great conspiracy of the Nobility.

Darnley was, like Riccio, a sacrifice to the Calvinistic nobles.

The murder of the King was eminently a political deed. The King was murdered by those who, from political reasons, had determined on his death at Craigmillar, but with the assistance and joint knowledge of a very great part of the nobles. Bothwell passed afterwards for the only murderer, simply because his share in the murder was the most certainly known, and because the material which furnishes the connected history of the affair had not been at all at any time critically examined.

later dates; and yet, nevertheless, in many respects, far superior to his surroundings.

*   *   *   *   *   *   *   *

In the night-time, and then only, placards were posted, and lamenting voices were heard, which, amid the darkness, proclaimed Bothwell and Mary guilty of the murder of Darnley. Since these originated with the faithless Morton, the principal accomplice in the crime, it was treachery towards Bothwell, and a breach of the agreement or "Bond," and a lie in so far as he, instead of naming himself, accused Mary Stuart, of whose participation in it—whatever her share in it, more or less, may have been—he could know nothing. Bothwell, enraged at this, swore to wash his hands in the blood of the slanderer if he could ferret him out. At all events the Earl was brave enough personally to press for an inquiry, and, in the Privy Council, sufficiently bold to sign the order for legal proceedings against himself. As a consequence, on the 12th April, he was declared free from this suspicion by a court which was composed principally of men privy to the murder,—a tribunal of which the proceedings have, with justice, always been regarded as a sheer comedy.

It should, however, never be forgotten, that if the proceedings were unjust, the blame is not to be laid upon Mary Stuart, since her Privy Council had drawn up the form of procedure exactly so that this result might follow, and the whole nobility, at that time, agreed with the Council; nay, more, the whole Parliament immediately ratified their decision. Only Murray got out of the affair by setting off for France three days previously thereto. After this events pressed on in more and more rapid succession, hastened by Bothwell's bold and unrestrained energy. *All, Mary among them, acted like puppets under the influence of his powerful personality.* To Huntley his estates were restored as the price of his sister's divorce from Bothwell.

The 19th April, at the closing of the Parliament, almost the whole of the nobility (under compulsion, as they afterwards maintained,—*an hundred men by* ONE) signed in the Ainsley Tavern a declaration that they were convinced of Bothwell's innocence; that they would defend him against every slanderer; and recommended him as the most worthy husband for the Queen.

If the Queen did not accede to Bothwell's urging that she should marry him at once, this may not have been from disinclination, but because she wished to defer the union for a little longer time for the sake of decency. He, however, in the feverish haste of disquietude, especially because he knew that any delay foreboded danger, determined to compel events by audacity, and, with her consent, bear her off on the 24th of April to his castle at Dunbar. This plan was carried out, and, after proceedings hastily instituted, the divorce between himself and his wife was declared on the 3d and 7th of May, and he married the Queen on the 15th of May, having been first raised to the dignity of Duke of Orkney. All this was done in perfect understanding with the entire nobility. There is something wild in this extreme haste, yet it should not be ascribed to Mary but to Bothwell. The consciousness and the consequences of his action impelled him energetically forward. Darnley's murder had been consummated in order to put aside a phantom King in perfect understanding with the "vast majority" of the highest aristocracy. Perhaps *from patriotism* Bothwell expected to rescue the country from boundless confusion, and alas! as the result proved, he had only hastened to confirm it.

Thus Bothwell had now become Consort of the Queen and Lord of the land. He stood so high that no one approached near to him. Did he now entertain a wish to ascend still higher, and, over the body of the infant prince, to open the way to the throne for himself or his descendants? His enemies maintain that this was so. He certainly wished *to get possession of the Prince. Was this with an evil design? There is not the smallest positive proof or indication to justify such an idea.* In any case he was already master, and lorded it only too energetically, but his highest degree of elevation is also the extreme turning-point, the high-tide mark of his henceforth swiftly ebbing fortune. Having completed his structure, the building founded on a rotten basis had to break up and fall to pieces. His very commanding nature hastened the catastrophe. Who knows if the other nobility, his betrayers, could have possibly thrown him down if he had bought himself powerful friends by bribing or paying them with property confiscated from his enemies, as was the rule of the times, or if he had become their obedient instrument, the tool of a PARTY and not the imperious master of his class, all classes? The Scots wanted nothing resembling a *real* King or ruler, and least of all an illegitimate one. Bothwell labored under the fatal error of believing he could use an irregularly acquired authority for good purposes. Doubtless he foreboded evil without knowing whence it would come. Suspicion must have entered his mind. He could not have entirely deluded himself into the belief he was to enjoy his acquisitions in peace, yet he was not meanly cunning enough to make out what actually did threaten him. *Hence his disquiet, his dark, gloomy spirit, which was not natural to him,* and this clearly explains—in connection with the jealousy inseparable from absorbing love—his apparent harshness to Mary after the marriage.

The storm broke suddenly, foreseen but not expected, and surprising him when it did come. Already between the 20th and 26th of May conferences of the nobles had taken place, with the object of dethroning the Queen and crowning James VI., who was but a year old. They soon signed a "Bond" against Mary and Bothwell. Lord Hume, Bothwell's old enemy, was to lead off. Liberton, in Midlothian, was indicated as the rendezvous for the 8th or 9th of June, and *all this occurred before Bothwell had even demanded the surrender of the Prince*, whom the Earl of Mar guarded in Stirling. This is the best proof that Bothwell's foes *knowingly maintained a falsehood when they averred that they rose only on account of Bothwell's demand for the custody of the year-old Prince and solely to protect the royal infant.* In one word, the party which elevated Bothwell,—that is, the party of his old enemies,—the false Murray, the foul Morton, *ce fin renard*, to use the most expressive phrase of Henry IV., Lethington, let him fall, and he fell. In the early part of June the Lords of the Border, Hume, Ker, Ferneherst, set themselves in motion. Bothwell issued a proclamation against them. Few resorted to his banners. The inhabitants of Edinburgh showed a dangerous discontent, so he departed in haste with Mary on the 6th June, 1567, for the purpose of going to Both-wick and collecting troops, leaving Edinburgh Castle in the hands of the double-dyed traitor Sir James Balfour. The City at once received Morton and the hostiles. That old wily conspirator was at the head, and, according to his party watch-word, the Queen was to be set at liberty. From whom? From her husband chosen by the very "Bond" now arrayed themselves against him and accepted by her? Bothwell had directed his levies to rendezvous at Melrose on the 15th June against the rebellious Borderers. The insurgents hoped to anticipate the royal rising. They surrounded Borthwick Castle in hopes of taking the Royal Pair, but Bothwell escaped, and somewhat later the Queen. She flew to rejoin her husband, and both took refuge in Dunbar. The insurgents, however, did not pursue, but first made sure of Edinburgh, and issued a proclamation on the 11th June that the Queen should be separated from Bothwell. Some faithful adherents at the same time gathered around her,—from two thousand to two thousand five hundred men. Here, again, Fate seemed to offer a solution. Had Mary delayed a few days, even her worst enemies admit the Bond against her would have dissolved of itself. But it was not to be. Bothwell's boldness precipitated the event. He thought only of conquering by force, but at Carberry Hill they came upon the enemy in greater force, double in numbers to his own. The troops were spiritless, the Queen undecided, Bothwell ardently wished a duel with Morton, who evaded it. In the hoary traitor's stead Lord Lindsay presented himself. The Queen forbade the meeting. The negotiations of the French ambassador, the promises of the knightly (so esteemed, but erroneously, as events proved) Kirkaldy of Grange, determined the Queen to give herself up, with full confidence, into the hands of the conspirators. Bothwell hastened away, accompanied by a few trusty adherents, under an understanding (as is asserted by his detractors) with the enemy. How these latter kept their promises and sent the Queen on the second day afterwards into prison at Lochleven, and forced her to abdicate and later to fly into England, is well known.

It is the especial business of this consideration to follow out, with exactness, the final fate of Bothwell.

The facts are manifoldly distorted; they envelop Bothwell like the opaque mists evoked by a magician, and in them this important personage again sinks into deep obscurity.

That the conspirators did not at once pursue and get him into their power may seem astonishing, but they knew that he had not followers enough to make him dangerous, and they did not care to take him at once. He might have brought too many things to light. However, they concluded on the 16th a new "Bond" for the prosecution of the Earl of Bothwell. Sir James Balfour, his immediate assistant in the undertaking, and the actual deviser of the plan for the murder of Darnley, now again threw in his lot among them and joined in their faithless design. Bothwell for reasons unknown left Dunbar, put to sea and fled to the North, and was finally forced by Fate into Denmark, where he died in prison. The particulars of this flight, however, have always been given in a very brief and unsatisfactory manner. Let us first hear Robertson :

"Bothwell fled to the Bishop of Murray, then to the Orkney Islands. Escaping thence with few followers he fell into the utmost need, and was forced into a kind of life which increased his infamy. He practiced piracy. Kirkland of Grange and Murray of Tullibardine being sent against him with some ships, surprised him as he lay at anchor. He was beaten, and with one ship fled to Norway. On the coast of this country he attacked a vessel. The Norwegians came to its relief, and, after a desperate fight, he and his companions were taken and treated as pirates. It was only from his being recognized that he was spared the death to which his companions were condemned. He died in prison, after ten years' confinement, having sunk at last into deep despondency and aberration of mind."

The true and false is here mingled in the most wonderful manner. According to this account, Bothwell died in the year 1577. Chalmers gives the year 1576, and many agree with him, but it is incontestable that he died in 1575, eight years after his flight. In proof of this, on the 24th November, 1575, Danzay, the French ambassador of Henry III., in Copenhagen, adds, after he has announced the death of the Danish Chancellor, Peder Oxe, who died on the 24th October, "and the Earl of Bothwell, a Scotchman, is also deceased."[9]

Besides this particular misrepresentation, Robertson's narrative is full of errors, accidental or willful. In fact, it has no chronology. This is owing perhaps to the very fact that it is founded on the falsehoods of Buchanan and Melvil, which have no basis whatever of truth, only of virulent consistent defamation.

It is particularly important to ascertain how long Bothwell remained in the Scottish waters, and when he was imprisoned in Denmark. If Danish Archives did not help to throw light upon the story,

[9] This dispatch is for the first time published in "*Nya Handlingar rorande Skandinaviens historia Stockholm*," 1824, xi., but it is almost totally unknown.

all would remain shrouded in darkness. Happily, these offer many pieces of information, which, however, have never yet been published in connection, and which only became perfectly accessible to Dr. Phil A. Petrick because the Keeper of the Archives of the King of Denmark, Privy Conference Counsellor, Dr. Wegener, had the kindness to send him, a few years since, a full collection of all the judicial processes, printed and unprinted, then lying in the Royal Danish Archives. To him, Dr. Wegener, as well as to his Excellency the German ambassador to Denmark, Heydebrand, and von de Lasa, especial thanks are due for similar assistance.

Especially valuable are the Minutes of the First Hearing that was given to Bothwell before the law officers at Bergen,—first published by Bergenhammer, in the translation of the History of Mary Stuart by von Gentz, Copenhagen, 1803.

This is of 23d September, 1567. His capture cannot have occurred long before. Only three months, therefore, have to be accounted for. First of all, Bothwell sailed between 30th June and 7th July with some (three or five) ships to the North, without being immediately followed (*i.e.*, he was not pursued until after the Outlawry of 26th June), accompanied by Lord Hay of Tallow, John Hepburn, and Bartoun,— who were subsequently executed 3d January, 1568,—Dalgleish, French Paris, and William Murray. Inch Keith was surrendered at the same time to the insurgents, but Dunbar held out to the 1st September. Bothwell could probably have made himself secure in the latter fortress, but he felt himself more free and safer on the high seas. He felt like the Douglas of old, " I would rather hear the lark sing (the sea-gull shriek) than the mouse squeak." At first he repaired to his great-uncle, Patrick Hepburn, Bishop of Murray, and passed a while at Spynis Castle, near Elgin. Christopher Rokesby, an English spy, proposed to Elizabeth's agent, Throckmorton, to murder Bothwell. Throckmorton referred him to the personally unprincipled Morton.

He was also with the Earl of Huntley at Strawboggyn in order to induce him to take up arms. He did not succeed in rousing his brother-in-law. Bothwell then hastened on to his Dukedom of Orkney. Here also treachery was predominant. His own vassal, Gilbert Balfour, brother of the Edinburgh traitor, Sir James Balfour, the real author of Darnley's murder, denied him entrance into his own Castle of Kirkwall. Things had now become perilous for him. Bothwell had to leave the Orkneys and endeavor to maintain himself in Shetland. He was still master of the sea. If Murray is to be believed he issued *letters of marque;* but only a blind enemy, not an impartial searcher after truth, can see *piracy* in this. A state of war existed, and, formally viewed, Bothwell's side of the question was the best, since he was not only Consort of the Queen and Duke of the Orcades, or Orkneys, but also Hereditary High Admiral of Scotland. Thus he stood with threefold strength in his own proper right. Whether about this time he attacked some hostile ships of his opponents is not known, but if he did do so he acted in accordance with the laws of war. He spared foreigners. There is yet existing in the Danish Archives the contract which Bothwell concluded on the 15th August, 1567, in the Harbor of "Upt Ness," near Sumborough Head, in Shetland, with the Bremen skipper, Gerdt Hemelengk, whom he found there with his vessel, the "Pelican." This he hired for two months at fifty crowns a month. This hiring or chartering is not contradicted, but corroborated by the Certificate of Olav Sinclair, Treasurer of Shetland, to Gerdt Hemelengk, made out the 15th September, to the effect that nothing had been paid up to that time. Moreover, the petition of Hemelengk to the Burgomaster and Council of Bremen, 3d March, 1568, states expressly that the Scottish Lord had induced—not compelled—him to sell his ship or to hire it out for two months. Such transactions are not the proceedings of a pirate.

The fight between Bothwell and Tullibardine and Kirkaldy is the more correctly to be assigned to the last days of August, since, probably, in consequence of the result of the encounter,—unfavorable to Bothwell,—Dunbar was surrendered to his enemies. Before the beginning of August, Bothwell's pursuers had not started. Kirkaldy was present at Lochleven at the time of the Queen's Abdication, 24th July, 1567. It was not determined in the Privy Council at Dunbar, at which Morton presided, until after 31st July to dispatch Tullibardine and Kirkaldy in pursuit of Bothwell. Indeed, the commission issued to them is of the 11th August: "To pursue the Earl and his accomplices by sea or land, with fire, sword, and all kind of hostility, and fence and hold courts of justice wheresoever they shall think good." The Bishop of Orkney, Adam Bothwell, the same who had performed Bothwell's marriage with Mary, and who was one of the Lords of Session (*i.e.*, Judges of the Supreme Court of Scotland), accompanied them. His co-operation was simply, perhaps, for the purpose of having a high judicial officer ready at hand to try and sentence and execute the outlawed Earl if he fell into the hands of his perfidious enemies.

Two engagements took place by Bressesund and by Ounst in Shetland. At the first place Bothwell's men were ashore. They cut the cables and proceeded to Ounst. Here, however, only one, not two, of Bothwell's ships were taken, and Tallow, Hepburn, Dalgleish, and others were captured, and at a later period executed. But the principal vessel, with a smaller one, escaped by reason of Kirkaldy's ship running on a sand-bank and remaining stuck fast thereon.

This brings this narrative to the ever hitherto befogged story of Bothwell's sojourn in Norway and Denmark. He was there arrested, NOT, *however, for piracy,* but for want of credentials. The whole history of this affair—which nevertheless even Mignet repeats—is clear ill-natured fable. Buchanan himself does not put it in his history, but in his famous " *Detectio.*" The whole story is utterly false. Bothwell did not attack a ship; the Norwegians did not come to the rescue; he was not accused of being a pirate; not one of his companions was indicted and executed. The record of the official trial expressly mentions that Christian Olborrig, Captain of the Danish ship of war " Bjornen," had detained two merchant vessels (*Pinken*, Pinks) because they had no sort of credential papers aboard. There is nothing in the proceedings about " piracy."

What is more and more important to the truth, Bothwell was not at first held as a prisoner. Erick Rosenkrantz, Commandant of Bergen, allowed him at his request to lodge at a hotel or tavern, and entertained him nobly and elegantly in the castle. He was virtually free. As he was in a very destitute condition, he looked out on going ashore for suitable clothing for himself and for his people. The Lady Anne, daughter of one Christopher Thrunndsen, provided it, and her he paid with the smaller of his two vessels (Pinks). The larger he said was (as has been hereinbefore mentioned) hired Bremen property, and since some doubted this, he left the vessel at Bergen. Bear in mind it is not Bothwell who states all this, but the Court and the sworn Referees of Bergen to their King, Frederic II. On this account the ships were not confiscated, but left at Bothwell's disposal, the best of proof, if any more were required, that he had not been and was not detained as a " pirate."

Soon after this Bothwell turns up in Copenhagen, apparently at liberty, yet possibly always under some degree of supervision. On the 12th November, 1567, he writes thence to Charles IX. of France that he had spoken to the French ambassador Danzay, and that he desired to go to France. In this letter *he commends himself to that monarch's kindness by recalling his ever-faithful services as Chamberlain and Captain of the Scottish Guards.* The letter appears to be written under no feeling of anxiety, and he does not even ask for mediation in favor of his being set free, and was, therefore, at liberty.

It is evident and naturally so that the Scottish government was exceedingly desirous of the extradition of Bothwell, whom they had with amusing haste declared before the Parliament, 20th December, 1567, guilty of high treason,—that is, before the same Parliament which in April of the same year with equal inconsistency had declared him guiltless; and it is clearly evident that the Scotch authorities were supported in their demand by Elizabeth, the protectress of (her " Spaniel") Murray. Nevertheless, these requisitions met with no success. In the first place, because King Frederic received no guaranty that the trial of Bothwell—before judges composed of his own actual accomplices in the crimes to be considered—would be conducted in an impartial manner;

and, in the second place, because the King himself was not persuaded of Bothwell's guilt, the more so in that the Earl was accused only in connection with Mary, who appeared to the King to be innocent. The negotiations in respect to Bothwell's extradition become clear enough from numerous documents which were exchanged on the subject, and which are preserved in the Royal Danish Archives. A portion of these have been printed. They only reveal, however, in a measure, partially clear ideas when they are gone through carefully in chronological order.

Even before the 30th September, when Murray, as Regent, wrote to King Frederic II., in the name of James VI., from Stirling, concerning Bothwell's extradition, Captain John Clark is said to have been sent as Envoy to Denmark to obtain either Bothwell's head or person. At all events, the letter of James VI. (Murray's) to Frederic II. treats of this, together with Clark's instructions of 25th August, 1568.[10] Schiern's date, 1567, must be an error, and the year instead be 1568.

[10] In order to comprehend the action of Frederic II. of Denmark (born 1534, succeeded to the crown 4th April, 1558, in regard to Bothwell), it is necessary to investigate the character of that king. According to his portrait in Fredericksborg " he looks the very pattern of decorum, although his face, red and puffy, tells of strong liquor." Indeed " Anders Bedel, the parson, in his funeral sermon declared had he abstained from wine bibbing he might have now been alive and in good health." Perhaps he liked Bothwell because he could drink deep; and " Scotland's proudest carl" is said to have drank his enemy, the Scottish envoy, Captain Clarke, to death in the prison-house common to both and the latter's eminent deserts. He was a *positive* man, that is, one unusually strong in his convictions. His nobility, courtiers, and officials had given him so much trouble, and he had experienced such continued treason or treachery and annoyances of " cabals" against his authority, that he had " lost all faith in men and fortune ;" and was accustomed to express his convictions in two ejaculations, the first, " My hope is in God alone," inscribed upon his tomb in the Cathedral at Roeskilde, which he so greatly beautified and endowed, and the second, " Faithful (or Trustworthy) is Wildpret or Wildbratt," his favorite hound, who " bit everybody but his royal master," to whom he always resorted for comfort in trouble. This second proverb, commonly written T. I. W. B., is still perpetuated in many places in Zealand, among others the carpets in the Castle of Fredericksborg, where this dog is represented with these letters on his collar. It is said that by the conjoined exclamations " My trust is in God alone," " Faithful is Wildpret," Frederic meant to signify that except in God and in the brute creation, the highest and the lowest, he had found nothing living in which he could confide. In spite of this partial misanthropy, he was a liberal prince, honest and pious, although straightlaced, if not bigoted to some degree in his views of religion. He was a zealous Protestant, but a strict sectarian, and " would allow of no dissent, no Calvinistic tendencies ; the Lutheran was the recognized religion of the land, and that people must hold to or nothing." He published a book of extracts from the Psalms, the Proverbs, and the common-sense teachings of Jesus, the son of Sirach, and had the Bible translated into the Icelandic. With all this he was not fond of people who differed from his views of the faith that was in him. Consequently, he may not have had full confidence in Bothwell on account of his loose ideas of living, although in one of his letters respecting the Scotch earl, 18th November, 1568, he designated him " Our pairticular Favorite." Whether Bothwell afterwards did anything to offend his puritanical sense of propriety is not shown and not known ;

The King answered Murray, on the 30th of December, that he could not give Bothwell up without great injustice, since the case was not clear, and his guilt was not proved. He intended to bring the case before the next Assembly of the Magnates in Denmark. Meanwhile, he would keep a good and strict watch over him.

Of the 13th November, 1567, appear the Instructions of Peder Oxe, the Chancellor, and of John Friis, as to the conduct to be observed towards Bothwell. A letter of Bothwell to Frederic II. fits on to this. The reply of Bothwell to Peder Oxe is of 18th November, 1567. Under date, the 28th December, 1567, is preserved the royal command for the incarceration of Bothwell at Malmö. Of the same date a memorial of Peder Oxe to Frederick II. and the answer to this, of 1st January, 1568.

On the 5th January, 1568, Bothwell was still in Copenhagen, but at this date imprisoned; because he, himself, mentions "The contumelies and indignities that I endure in this prison," whence he ad-

but as Bothwell was very impulsive, although it is intimated that 16th June, 1573, there occurred for the first time a radical change in his treatment of Bothwell, and then his real strict captivity began, nothing is more probable than that Bothwell's fiery nature incited him to revolt against the injustice and constraint to which he was subjected, and kings do not like the truth or outspoken sentiments contrary to their own.

It may be that love—which interferes with the lives of most men and renders them happy or the reverse, love which did not run smoothly—had a great deal to do with making Frederic what he was, and the usual antidote to such poison is wine. " Frederic II. was, when we consider the age he lived in, a right-minded, honorable man. In early life he was much attached to a young and beautiful girl, Dagmar Hardenberg by name, who, though of noble birth, belonged to no princely house ; make her his queen he could not, and he was too high-principled to take advantage of her youth, so he remained a bachelor until he was thirty-eight years of age, when, yielding to the entreaties of his advisers, he, much against his will, contracted an alliance with the Princess Sophia of Mecklenburg. Tradition relates how Dagmar was present at the coronation of the queen, which took place in the Frue Kirke of Copenhagen, but, overcome by her feelings, fainted away, was carried out of the church, and died shortly after broken-hearted. Two daughters were the produce of Frederic's marriage, and, in despair at the non-arrival of an heir to the crown, he began to regret he had yielded to the desire of his nobles."

Petrick assures his readers that the last four years of Bothwell's life are a blank. Consequently, everything in regard to them is speculation, except it is averred that, even after he was committed to the Castle of Dragsholm, he "nevertheless got permission to go a hunting," 383, 1. Undoubtedly, however, as Schiern quotes from a letter of the French Ambassador Dancey, 28th June, 1573, " Up to this time the King of Denmark had treated the Earl of Bothwell kindly enough, but within a few days he has had him transferred to a very evil and close prison."

It may be interesting to know that Frederic II. was patron of many learned men, and among these Tycho Brahe, the celebrated astronomer, to whom he committed the sculptural adornment of the Royal Mausoleum at Roeskilde, and he protected Melancthon and other German Reformers. He it was rebuilt Kronborg, the famous castle near Elsmere, so well known to the admirers—and who are not?— of Hamlet. It is said, " Had Shakespeare searched the world round he never could have selected so fitting a locality for the ghost scene as the ramparts of Kronborg."

dressed his first Memorial to the Danish King, and defends himself
with great skill, even against the accusation as to the murder of
Darnley.

This the Bannatyne Club in Edinburgh, 1828, published from a
copy which Bothwell gave to the French ambassador, Danzay, and
which is kept in the library of the Royal Castle of Drothingholm, in
Sweden. Labanoff used a copy, which is preserved by the family of
d'Esneval, and which is accompanied with some remarks by Bothwell.
This second exemplar was, perhaps, sent through Danzay to Charles
IX. of France.

On the 29th March, 1568, Westminster, Elizabeth wrote to Frederic II., "Commissioners will arrive from Scotland in order to extra-
dite Bothwell;" indorsed, "Received on the 21st April." The
original, in the Royal Archives, is not printed.

On the 4th May, 1568, Elizabeth urges Frederic II. afresh and
pretty energetically to consent to the extradition. On the 16th July,
1568, James VI. wrote to Frederic II. in regard to the approaching
mission of Clark in regard to Bothwell. By this time Frederic appears to have become somewhat uncertain and desirous of obtaining
external authority or advice for his action, since he invites, under date
9th August, 1568, different German princes to furnish their opinions
as regards the extradition. The answers of the German princes came
in under the 25th, 27th August, 1st, 11th, 19th September.

Another letter of James VI. (by Murray), of the 28th August,
1568, was dispatched to Frederic II., written on the occasion of the
departure of Axel Wiffert. Clark's mission was not altogether without
result. On the 30th October, 1568, he gave a certificate of the receipt
of Nicholas Howbert (Hubert), called "French Paris," and of William
Murray, both accused of the murder of Darnley. The first was gentleman in waiting to Bothwell, afterwards to Mary. His examinations
and declarations under date of 9th, 10th of August, 1569, in St. An-
drews have been often printed, but they seem to have been tampered
with. Hubert was executed (judicially murdered) on the 15th August,
1569. Of the fate of William Murray nothing is heard.

After Clark's departure, Bothwell's situation seems to have been
improved, 1569; and no demand made for him. He was placed on a
respectable footing. Of date 2d March, 1569, appears an official entry
regarding "velvet and silk for Bothwell."

According to Chalmers, Bothwell gave in this year a letter and
plenary commission (irrevocable power of attorney?) to Lord Boyd
to declare his assent to a divorce from Mary Stuart. This letter was
accessible until 1746, among the family papers of the descendants of
Lord Boyd. About this time the Regent Murray was assassinated in
Scotland, 23d January, 1570. The Earl of Lenox, father of Darnley,
was then elevated to the office of Regent of Scotland on the 12th July,

1570, and at once fresh demands were again made for the extradition of Bothwell.

Under date of 17 July, James VI. (by Lenox) writes to Frederic II., and begs him by no means to free Bothwell out of respect to those who desire to represent the Earl as innocent. This was received in Copenhagen 7th August. The letter of Peder Oxe and Johan Friis to Frederic II. of 22d June, 1570, and Frederic's answer of 24th June, 1570, appear to treat of this advice. Elizabeth joined in the request of Lenox, 3d August, 1570, and as Clark, who had been sent out, was represented as being a disreputable person by Bothwell, the English Queen became responsible for his honor. To the same purpose, August, 1570, James VI. (by Lenox) addressed himself to Frederic II. Nevertheless, as Clark was not deemed reputable, his services appear to be considered useless, and, in December of the same year, a special ambassador from Scotland was sent out,—Thomas Buchanan; not the Historical writer, but his nephew. He, on the 14th December, in a long Latin address, handed in in manuscript on the 16th December, asks the King, Frederic, for a final extradition of Bothwell, and under the 31st December, concisely begs the Danish monarch for an answer. The original, not printed, is in the Royal Danish Archives.

Under date 9th March, 1570, the momentous reply of Frederic to Thomas Buchanan, as regards the demand that Bothwell should either be executed in Denmark or extradited to Scotland, the King answers that Bothwell's guilt is *not clear,* since the captive Earl denies participation in the crime of which he is accused; setting forth that he has already been once pronounced innocent in Scotland; and demanding that at proper time he may have judicial trial by battle, or else a new legal trial either in Denmark or in Scotland, where the impartiality of the judges can be guaranteed. It is undeniable that Bothwell's demands are as just as they are clear, and they afford decisive proofs of sense and courage. He likewise requires the same guaranty, together with other safeguards (political), that the extradition shall create no precedent, before he (himself) will consent to a surrender. He desires an answer before the 24th August. Clark, sent out to obtain Bothwell's extradition, was now, for his own acts, justly incarcerated, and died in the Danish prison that held his intended victim.

Buchanan, the Scottish envoy, received this letter on the 12th March, and answered it on the 19th. He at once accepted the proposals, and wished that Frederic II. would himself formulate the guaranty, and recounts once more the crimes of which Bothwell was accused, among them the abduction of the innocent Queen. Take notice that the same parties who were actively protesting her innocence in Denmark, accused her in England of participation in the murder of Darnley by Bothwell, and of being an accessory to her own abduction by the latter. Buchanan states he demands Bothwell's delivery for trial, " Because he had publicly used force with the Queen, . . . that most potent Princess, richly endowed by God with the highest gifts, to be regarded among the chief of princes on account of her peculiar virtues and rarest endowments both of body and of mind." He, Both- . well, " this natural monster," is said to have enticed [or deluded] her " by fascinations, filtres, incantations, and sorcery, with other evil arts."

In this way the extradition was virtually decided on, and Elizabeth did not need, under date of 22d March, 1570, to address a fresh epistle to Frederic II. in which she demands that Bothwell be sent to England. But the guarantees to be demanded were not so easily defined in a way to content the cautious and honorable King of Denmark, and the friends of Mary Stuart employed every means to hinder this. The extradition was to take place on the 24th August, Danzay had consented, but La Mothe Fénelon, French Ambassador of Charles IX. in London, conjured his master under date of 20th June, 1571, most earnestly not to permit this to be done. King Charles IX. appears to have concurred with his Representative and to have given Danzay such instructions as delayed the dangerous crisis. The letters of Danzay to Charles IX. and Catharine de Medici of 2d April, 15th July, and 1st September, 1571, are filled with the subject. James VI. (by Lenox, under date of 5th July, received 31st July) urges Frederic II. afresh to fulfill his promise. The original is printed in the Royal Danish Archives. The thunderstorm was gathering dangerously over Bothwell's head, but proper guarantees—for verbal promises amounted to nothing—were not furnished, and the King does not seem to have once again asked for them. Then suddenly—all is silent!—a great gap of four years occurs: the extradition did not take place. For what reason?

On the 4th September, 1571, a fresh murder took place in Scotland. " Lenox, the Regent, was killed by [the chivalrie (*sic*)] Kirkaldy of Grange, Huntley, and others." Great discords followed. The Earl of Mar became Regent, and had enough upon his hands at home to prevent his troubling himself about the unfortunate Bothwell. Mar's uprightness—acknowledged by all parties—did not avail to save him. He died [by poison (?) suspected] 29th October, 1572. To him as Regent succeeded the most dangerous man in Scotland, the Earl of Morton; he, who was an accomplice in the murder of the King (Darnley), the best of proofs that the general hatred against Bothwell was grounded on other and more ignoble motives than a desire for justice. Bothwell now had rest from his enemies. A single letter of James VI., 1575, reminds Frederic II., merely incidentally, of these negotiations. The King must have understood that a guaranty for a just examination of the case in Scotland was out of the question at this time, and have recognized that the accusations against Bothwell were at least partially calumnious. Notwithstanding—why is incomprehensible—Bothwell did not obtain his liberty.

Over and above all these false charges Bothwell is said to have been accused of the abduction of different respectable young ladies. There is nothing of the sort contained in the Danish Archives, and for this he could have been impeached only in Denmark. Thus the latter charges are decidedly false.

Almost all maintain that Bothwell lost his senses in the prison. If such had been the case it would not have been wonderful; indeed, if true, it would present a proof of his active spirit and original nobility of soul. That he became subject to melancholy from such a startling change of fortune and from regret is not unlikely, but truth compels the decision that even this statement is not proved.

Next in order comes the consideration of the existence of a Testatament [or Will, so styled] of Bothwell, a statement which he is said to have made upon his death-bed. Teulet printed it in French and in English. The former was at first published by Keith after a copy contemporary (with the original) in the Scottish College at Paris, which is now lost; the latter after a contemporary copy. Teulet considers them false,—founded on very weak grounds. Labanoff proves that a Testament really did exist. A letter of Foster to Walsingham, 15th June, 1581, gives evidence of it. In any case the Testament was used against Morton, when, in 1584, he was proved guilty of the murder of Darnley, and for this, as well as many other misdeeds, was executed. It was forwarded by King Frederic II. to Queen Elizabeth, but not made public by her, and its contents kept from the knowledge of Mary. At the same time, although Petrick believes that something of the kind did exist, the careful Doctor is compelled to pronounce the testimony brought forward by Teulet to be spurious, especially so, since the two pretended copies of it do not exactly agree. The Parisian version makes the "Paris Brawe von Schloss Veseut" [Brahe of Vidskovle, a chateau near Christianstad, now in Sweden] to be present; the English does not. The French version includes a greater number among the murderers of Darnley than the English. According to the latter, Bothwell cannot recollect all. In other respects they disagree in many points. But of more importance are completely false statements of facts. The Confession declares that my Lord Robert, Prior of Holyrood, Earl of Orkney, was among the murderers. He, however, was precisely the one who warned Darnley. For the same reason Crawford could not have been present, since he was a jealous partisan and friend of Darnley. Bothwell knew this perfectly well, and would not have stultified himself with such errors or inventions.

That Bothwell should represent himself as practicing sorcery is scarcely credible. He is said to have confessed to having abducted divers ladies from France, England, Denmark, and Germany. This is incredible. If he had done so they must have turned up somewhere, and certainly it would have been brought against him and Mary. His enemies had not so much delicacy as to be silent respecting such a charge if true. As far as Denmark is concerned, it is manifestly disproved. Again, it cannot be believed that he ever abducted two sisters at one time; that he "has deceived tway (two) of the Burgomaster's daughters of Lubeck with many others." A Burgomaster of Lubeck, in those times, was not the man to go unrevenged and sit down quietly without making proper reclamation and compelling some wild kind of justice most satisfying and satisfactory to himself.

More weighty, however, than even these improbabilities presents themselves in that the writings are dated from Malmö,[11] and almost all later (even the best) authors agree to make Bothwell die in Malmö, 1577 or 1576. Bothwell, however, died in Dragsholm, a solitary castle on a tongue of land in Northwest Zeeland, in the beginning of November, 1575.

When he was transported to the prison in Dragsholm has not been ascertained, although it was probably after Frederic II.—subsequent to the end of the year 1571—had made up his mind not to surrender him. And, although the tower in Malmö is shown as the place where Bothwell died, this is only another instance of how little even the natives have been instructed on the subject or know about it.

Such was the end—dark and almost mythical—of a man who, for a time, controlled the fate of Scotland, and who, as the third husband of the most beautiful (so esteemed) Queen,—when once he dragged her along with him down the precipitous pathway of his (or their mutual) passions,—exerted a most fatally decisive influence over her. Such was the end of the man who just came short of winning the Crown, and who, not altogether unjustly, paid penance for his rapid rise by a more rapid fall. He is one of the most noteworthy and instructive personalities in history, and his career is especially impressive—purely tragic—by reason of the close connection of guilt, greatness, daring, and downfall. A change of fortune could in no instance have occurred more quickly and decidedly than in his case, and he must bear the full responsibility of his deeds. These his best friends do not wish to excuse where they do not merit excuse. His great political faults were a want of mistrust in believing that his enemies were capable of such infernal hypocrisy and mutual change of mind or treachery, and a credulity through which he allowed himself to be

---

[11] Malmö, formerly a place of strength, then belonging to Denmark, now in Sweden, on the eastern shore of the Sound (*Ore Sund*) nearly opposite and east-southeast of Copenhagen, but sixteen miles distant. Dragsholm (Draxholm) is in an entirely different direction. It is on the same island with Copenhagen, but fifty miles at least to the west by north. To confound the two places is either the result of utter ignorance or else of intentional misrepresentation.

used by these traitors as a tool even against himself, and a moral and tragic guilt,—by which he was led to conceive that by a murder he would be able to bring about an improvement of affairs, however much this may have been needed, in his native country. Conceding all this, when, afterwards, ignorance and malicious falsehood seek to distort his memory beyond recognition, the real facts of his unhappy life deserve so much the more to be brought prominently forward and demonstrated with clearness in the light of truth. It is undeniable that he *had brilliant qualities, mental and physical; that he possessed an open, liberal nature; that he was of unchangeable fidelity, high-hearted and generous.* He was not, it is true, without the frivolous characteristics of the French and the wilder nature or disposition of a Scotchman of his time; pomp-loving and prodigal; a child of civil war; brave and ready to fight, yet only inclined for open and violent action, not cunning or underhand dealing. He does not rise above his time, but he looms up as one of the most powerful in it, a born master-spirit, whose tragical position lies in that it stirred him up to take by force what seemed to be or was eventually denied him by Fate, and in that he thought by *a crime—which can be proved to have been the only one of his life—to restore peace to his deeply disturbed country.* He is a speaking proof that even to the greatest such a deed of violence can eventuate only for evil. In any event, he is worthy of a far better remembrance in history than that which is allowed to him. The verdict against him is utterly baseless, although up to this very day calumnies, repeated with virulence and anxious care, have been allowed to distort and conceal the facts in regard to him. That bitter wrong has been done to James Hepburn, Earl of Bothwell, can be shown from original authorities hitherto disregarded or kept out of sight, and whoever has read with care this vindication of the brave Earl must be convinced that amid the black flock of ravenous Scottish nobility in the sixteenth century, he appears, as Dr. Petrick observes, like that *rara avis*, a *White Crow.*

In conclusion, the verse (13) of Psalm lxviii. might justly, in many respects, be applied to the third husband of Mary Stuart, that "Though ye have lain among the pots," or, as the Walloon Commentator, Martin, translates it, "amid cinders and refuse,—the aristocratic generation among and with whom he had to act,—ye shall be [or appear] as the wings of a dove covered with silver, and her feathers of yellow gold."

www.ingramcontent.com/pod-product-compliance
Lightning Source LLC
Chambersburg PA
CBHW021526090426
42739CB00007B/800